11063456?

Mastering Civic Engagement:

A Challenge to Museums

AAM gratefully acknowledges the generous financial
support for the Museums & Community Initiative provided by
The Wallace Reader's Digest Funds.

Additional support was received from
The Ford Foundation,
The John S. and James L. Knight Foundation,
and The Nathan Cummings Foundation.

The American Association of Museums, as the national service organization representing the American museum community, addresses the needs of museums to enhance their ability to serve the public interest. AAM disseminates information on current standards and best practices and provides professional development for staff to ensure that museums contribute to public education in its broadest sense and protect and preserve our cultural heritage. Since its founding in 1906, AAM has grown to more than 15,900 members, including over 11,000 museum professionals and trustees, 1,900 corporate members, and 3,000 museums.

Mastering Civic Engagement: A Challenge to Museums

Copyright © 2002, American Association of Museums, 1575 Eye St. N.W., Suite 400, Washington, DC 20005; www.aam-us.org. All rights reserved. This book may not be reproduced, in whole or in part, in any form, except for brief passages by reviewers, without written permission from the publisher.

Design: LevineRiederer Design

Library of Congress Cataloging-in-Publication Data
Mastering civic engagement : a challenge to museums.
     p. cm.
Includes index.
 ISBN 0-931201-81-0
 1. Museums--Management. 2. Museums--Social aspects. 3.
Museums--Political aspects. 4. Museum visitors. 5. Community
development. I. American Association of Museums.
 AM7 .M37 2002
 069--dc21

                                  2002023262

Mastering Civic Engagement:

A Challenge to Museums

AMERICAN ASSOCIATION OF MUSEUMS

© 2002 American Association of Museums
1575 Eye St. N.W., Suite 400
Washington, DC 20005

TABLE OF CONTENTS

Points of View:
Reimagining Museums' Civic Potential

FOREWORD

. . . .

Today, we are told, the world is a different place than it was in mid-2001. But is it really? Or have we simply been reminded of the elementary yet profound truth that community matters?

Mastering Civic Engagement: A Challenge to Museums asks us to revisit the power of community and consider what assets museums contribute to the shared enterprise of building and strengthening community bonds. This book is a call to action, and every museum will have a highly individual response to its content.

For the American Association of Museums, *Mastering Civic Engagement* is a call to action as well. As the Museums & Community (M&C) Initiative, the basis for this book, proceeds, AAM is committed to supporting museums as they develop new strategies for civic engagement; strengthening our high-level relationships with national civic organizations; and working with funding organizations and public decision makers to ensure that museums have the resources to pursue and practice civic engagement.

American museums have unparalleled intellectual resources and a distinguished legacy of public service. People trust museums, and—as M&C has confirmed—communities are eager to work with them. *Mastering Civic Engagement* will inspire a different kind of inquiry in each museum, with different purposes. But, as Janet Gallimore, director of the Lake County Discovery Museum and M&C task force member, explains, in 2010 all museums should be able to say, "We have learned how to listen; we have become agents of dialogue; and we have lifted the human spirit."

Lou Casagrande
President, The Children's Museum, Boston
Chair, AAM Board of Directors, May 2002-May 2004

PREFACE
· · · · · · · · ·

As immediate past chair and current chair of the AAM Board of
Directors, we write in grateful recognition of the accomplishments and
abiding future importance of the Museums & Community Initiative.
Signaled in Rick's inaugural remarks at the 1998 AAM Annual Meeting in
Los Angeles and overseen by Freda since 2000, no undertaking of the
association in recent history has charted more significant substantive
territory in the museum community. Both of us are indebted to the gifted
and thoughtful leadership of Bob Archibald, who chaired the Museums &
Community Initiative National Task Force, as well as to those many others
within and without our community whose insight, imagination, and
dedication fueled the initiative's progress.

We have taken great pride in AAM's previous work to move the museum
community forward in anticipation of changing and complex societal
dynamics and developments in America. For the past two decades, beginning
with *Museums for a New Century* in 1984, the association consistently has
attempted to pose the questions museums of the 21st century should be
asking, as well as some of the possible answers and responses. AAM's
publications, *Excellence and Equity: Education and the Public Dimension of
Museums* and *New Visions for Museums*, provided both theoretical and
practical thought and advice about the wider roles museums can play in
better serving the communities of which they are a part.

We believe that the Museums and Community Initiative is pinned on this
distinguished legacy, but at the same time moves the discussion a critical
step forward into the future of the museum field and of the country. In
important respects, AAM's previous work on these subjects has focused on

encouraging museums to look outward toward the communities they are intended to serve and make their assets of information, collections, and expert human resources more broadly accessible to increasingly diverse publics. The Museums & Community Initiative, however, concentrates on the possibilities of making what previously has been essentially a unilateral relationship fundamentally bilateral in nature by extending an invitation to those in the broader community beyond the museum's four walls. The potential results of this change in dynamics are significant and substantial and create an environment in which the place of museums in their communities could be transformed, making them ever more responsive, integral, and valuable to their communities.

In the end, the Museums & Community Initiative counsels a process rather than patented blueprints or molds. The museum community represents and reflects a highly diverse set of institutions, and questions relating to the relationships between these important places and the communities they serve thus will be answered in correspondingly different ways. At the dawn of the 21st century, however, museums—hopefully as vital cultural and social institutions in a changed and rapidly changing society—are constrained to ask and to listen. In doing so, we believe that these wonderful places will remain essential and connective threads in the fabric of a great nation.

Freda Nicholson
President Emeritus
Discovery Place, Inc.
Charlotte, N.C.
Chair, AAM Board of Directors, 2000-2002

W. Richard West
Director
National Museum of the American Indian
Smithsonian Institution,Washington, D.C.
Chair, AAM Board of Directors, 1998-2000

INTRODUCTION
. . . .

By Robert R. Archibald

When W. Richard West, then chair of AAM's board of directors, asked me to chair the association's Museums & Community Initiative (M&C), I was thrilled. I accepted immediately—not because I had special insights into relationships between museums and their visitors, but because I knew that Rick was giving me an unparalleled opportunity to educate myself about the evolution of new and dynamic relationships between museums and the communities they exist to serve. I knew, too, that implicit in the structure of the initiative was the chance to listen to both museum professionals and engaged citizens from a multiplicity of backgrounds discuss the potential of museums to collaboratively construct new relationships that can contribute to community life.

My perceptions of museums and their possibilities were transformed as the initiative's six dialogues proceeded and I pondered the issues that were raised by the participants in Providence, Tampa, Los Angeles, Detroit, Wichita, and Bellingham. Gradually common issues, questions, opportunities, and themes emerged. I came to see that there is no proto-type, no cookie cutter for how museums define themselves and serve people. In fact, rich diversity is the dominant characteristic of museums. As we listened to the participants in the dialogue cities, it also became obvious that many museums and communities are engaged in marvelously successful experiments from which all of us can learn. It was evident that there are changing sets of public expectations to which museums will have to respond in some way. Finally, I realized that the dialogues and the whole initiative were not about museums developing new programs, exhibitions, collections, interpretations, or marketing plans. Instead, the conversations were about process, about how museums will go about the business of being museums, whether they are for general or specialized audiences, or focused on art, history, science, or a more specific subject. M&C is neither a new recipe for what museums do nor a one-sized shoe into which each institution must be crammed. Rather it is about a process through which museums and communities can redefine new mutual relationships that will vary from community to community and museum to museum.

....

How can we really allow communities to own museums?

....

The M&C dialogues were heavily weighted in favor of community representation. We did this so that museum people could not dominate the conversation. More than half of the participants in each of the dialogues were corporate leaders, educators, social service representatives, philanthropists, politicians, and other community opinion leaders. In all the dialogues, participants came up with many ideas for collaborations. Some were far-fetched, others traditional. But many were imaginative and intensely collaborative, involving not only museums but also an eclectic assortment of other community-based organizations with intersecting interests. At the conclusion of each dialogue, the ideas were presented to the entire group and reactions were solicited.

My own "eureka" moment occurred in reflective hours in the weeks after the dialogues were completed. Two exchanges symbolize what I learned from the process. In Los Angeles, a young man stopped me during a break. He explained that he directed a large social service organization that served people who were indigent. "What," he queried, "can museums do for my clients?" I mentally scrambled to think of museum programs and exhibitions that fit the bill. I could think of a few, but they were just haphazard examples at far-flung museums. As I struggled to find a way to give an encouraging answer, I turned the question around. "What if we viewed museums as an assemblage of assets: staff, physical facilities, collections, disciplinary and programmatic expertise, and community-gathering places, places of safety?" I asked. "If museum staff and your clients met, and we put our assets on the table and discussed how they might be arranged for the benefit of your clients, can you anticipate ways that they might be of value?" His response? "Of course." I realized that the ability of museums to expand community service depends upon the creation of new and really collaborative relationships, where we do not presume to know what audiences need. In these new relationships we will regard ourselves as reservoirs of information and expertise and will relinquish our traditional authoritarian roles in favor of new responsibilities as both resources and facilitators of dialogue about those things that matter most to people.

The other exchange occurred during the meeting in Tampa, where the 100 or so participants broke into small groups to discuss and design community-museum collaborations. One museum person questioned an imaginative suggestion, declaring "My institution could not and would not implement such a program. That initiative falls outside the scope of our mission." While that particular objection was not often repeated, it was apparent to me during all of the dialogues that the obstacles to new community-based collaborative relationships were not external. Never did I hear community representatives express any opposition to the idea that museums and their communities should develop collaborative, transparent relationships founded upon an axiom of shared authority. In fact, the opposite was true. Some community representatives even expressed tremendous frustration with museums that "talked the talk" but refused to "walk the real walk."

When expressed, the museum opposition to change in its community relationships was based on mission, best practices, presumptions of authority, and specialized expertise that could not be understood or exercised without academic training and pertinent experience. But many museum representatives embraced the possibilities of taking more active community-oriented roles and presented numerous marvelous examples of how a variety of institutions were embracing new roles and possibilities. At the Wichita dialogue, Rick West used a wonderful word. "Museums have long pursued outreach as a means of reaching new audiences," he said. "But now is the time for museums to consider *inreach*. How will museums adopt processes that encourage communities to reach into museums and significantly influence agendas?"

How can we really allow communities to own museums? Can we who work in museums learn to share authority over meanings ascribed to our collections and over the programs we choose to present? In other words, can we share our assets?

Our nation, and indeed much of the world, has changed a great deal in the past 50 years. Previously silenced voices insist upon being heard. Traditional sources of authority in our communities have lost much of their clout—both because citizens insist on participating in decisions that affect their lives and because of economic, political, and corporate change. Corporations cannot afford deep attachments to any one place in a global economy. Often their bases of customers, employees, and shareholders are international, and their executives pride themselves on their ability to do business from anywhere. Power in our communities is moving from older, more hierarchical forms to broad-based citizen coalitions. Decision-making processes in most communities are becoming democratic and inclusive; increasingly, those who will be affected are insisting on involvement in the decision-making process at the outset, even before the options are defined.

....

How can museums acknowledge the fact that it is those embedded memories that imbue objects with significance?

....

How will museums respond to these changed social dynamics? How will they find ways to accommodate community desires for meaningful roles in the presentation and interpretation of art, history, and science?

Perhaps this publication will provide some answers. It is presented in three parts. "Mastering Civic Engagement: A Report from the American Association of Museums," by Ellen Hirzy, M&C's consulting writer, provides a context and a starting point for museums. Rather than prescribe solutions or recommend actions, it urges museums to establish their own frameworks for inquiry, innovation, and action. This report also examines the historical perspective for AAM's exploration of museums and community, describes the qualities of museums as civic enterprises, and suggests questions that can guide inquiry about civic engagement. "A Framework for Civic Engagement" includes four essays from non-museum vantage points, written by Christopher T. Gates, president, National Civic League; Maria-Rosario Jackson, senior research associate, Urban Institute; Daniel Kertzner, program coordinator, Massachusetts Cultural Council; and Mariam Noland, president, and Katie M. Goatley, program officer, Community Foundation of Southeastern Michigan. In "Points of View," 10 people who participated in community dialogues reflect on the real work of civic engagement—on the ground in towns and cities throughout the nation.

Obstacles to change are often internal to our institutions. Many of the best practices that museums and the disciplines they encompass have developed, painstakingly and with great effort over many years, buttress the status quo. Sometimes these best practices are so embedded in the axioms of our work that it is nearly impossible to recognize them as obstacles. A few years ago, while visiting my hometown, I went to the local museum and asked to see my grandmother's wedding dress. "You cannot see it because it is not on exhibit," I was told. "You will have to make an appointment in advance." I wonder how many times my own institution has responded in a similar way. I understand the reasoning; we have spent many years dealing with fuzzy acquisition records of past decades and now strive to enforce the standard that museums must have clear title to their collections. Yet I have a different relationship to my grandmother's wedding dress than do the museum staff and the general public. That dress symbolizes the vows between my grandparents that made my own birth possible. How can museums acknowledge that historical collections often embody people's most personal possessions and memories, and the fact that it is those embedded memories that imbue objects with significance?

From my experience at the Missouri Historical Society, I know that there are many in the St. Louis community who view my own institution with suspicion because they and their histories have traditionally been excluded. Many have little reason to trust us with their treasured objects or to determine what will be said about them or how they will be used in the museum. Deeds of gift that insist that the donor assign all rights to the museum, including the right to dispose of the object, undermine efforts to construct new relationships based on collaboration, shared authority, and, perhaps especially, mutual trust. Our acquisition policies are but one obstacle to new community relationships. Certainly, wholesale abandonment of the practices we have painstakingly developed is neither possible or desirable. However, we ought to understand how internal processes, procedures, and assumptions about authority and expertise determine the potential of our relationships with those we exist to serve.

How can we do our work differently in order to reach our potential?

Museums face unprecedented opportunities to exert even greater influence in society. We are becoming places of dialogue, advocates of inclusion, places of values, and incubators of community. Without straying from our foundations, we can become places where consensus evolves around fundamental questions faced by people in every age. What is beautiful and what is ugly? What have we done well, what have we done poorly, and how can we do better? What is good, what is evil, and how do we know the difference? And how can we do our work differently in order to reach our potential? The answers will be different for every community and every museum. Change is a process, and the Museums & Community Initiative is about the process of change and about the process of inclusion as a means of community engagement. The processes will be similar but the outcomes will be as diverse as museums and their communities.

In November 2001 I stood among the antiquities in the first-floor galleries of the Metropolitan Museum of Art in New York. I was absolutely overwhelmed with feelings of connections to all people throughout time and the emotional realization of shared humanity that transcends both time and place. Here I found incontrovertible confirmation that people in the past were just like me in their creation and appreciation for beauty, their concern with mortality and the quest for immortality, and their search for happiness. Here was the enduring essence of museums, the preserved essence of human achievement and life on the surface of this wandering planet. Here was proof of the best that humans can achieve. Close to the shadows of the Sept. 11 tragedy, the Met is a spectacular reminder that good stands in contrast to evil, beauty to ugliness, and right to wrong. In the midst of a process to redefine the potential of museums and their relationships with people outside of their walls, we cannot and will not lose sight of the fundamental ideas and long-standing strengths that illuminate and give credibility to the work that museums do and the solace and transcendent experiences that they provide.

Robert R. Archibald, Ph.D., is president and CEO, Missouri Historical Society, St. Louis, and chair, Museums & Community Initiative National Task Force.

Exploring Museums & Community

MASTERING CIVIC ENGAGEMENT: A REPORT FROM THE AMERICAN
ASSOCIATION OF MUSEUMS *by Ellen Hirzy* | **9**

MASTERING CIVIC ENGAGEMENT: A REPORT FROM THE AMERICAN ASSOCIATION OF MUSEUMS

By Ellen Hirzy

Every museum has a deeply rooted connection with its community that is uniquely its own. However far reaching its collections and scholarship or the diversity of its audiences, a museum's particular community context anchors it, revitalizes its mission and sense of purpose, and enriches its understanding of what is possible to accomplish. Deceptively simple actions shape and support this connection: creating and tending a community garden with senior citizens and fifth-graders from a neighborhood school; transforming the museum's imposing entrance into the community's front porch; opening the museum as a place to find comfort after a devastating national tragedy.

Civic engagement occurs when museum and community intersect—in subtle and overt ways, over time, and as an accepted and natural way of doing business. The museum becomes a center where people gather to meet and converse, a place that celebrates the richness of individual and collective experience, and a participant in collaborative problem solving. It is an active, visible player in civic life, a safe haven, and a trusted incubator of change. These are among the possibilities inherent in each museum's own definition and expression of community.

Across professions and institutions throughout society, a vigorous exploration and reinvention of civic role is under way. Power and decision making are shared more broadly than ever before, giving citizens both expanded obligations and unparalleled opportunities. Where information and access were once tightly controlled and civic action could be carefully orchestrated, there are now diverse perspectives and voices engaged in shaping the quality of community life. The quest for understanding what community means and how to build a civil society are focal points of popular and academic discussion. Across the political spectrum, perspectives vary on the meaning and practical applications of the debate.[1] But the common ground is the belief that building community is essential, that people and organizations are just beginning to find new approaches to working together, and that we must transform our institutions—including our cultural institutions—as we move forward.

Museums have substantial potential as civic enterprises that contribute to building and sustaining community, and they are ready to pursue this potential. As stewards and as educators, museums are dedicated to excellence. They are respected as unsurpassed sources of intellectual capital, the objects and ideas that are the raw material of the museum experience. They also are respected for the exceptional ways in which they share their intellectual capital with the public, as educators and as sources of inspiration and wonder. Museums engender great confidence, and Americans trust them wholeheartedly as objective resources.[2]

The logical next step for museums is to learn and master the process of civic engagement. This task is critical to their evolution, their relevance, and their survival. Museums have a civic role beyond that of cultural symbol, economic engine, and provider of educational experiences. Other organizations and people in communities are confident that museums can fill this role. Most museums, however, are just beginning to approach and understand this notion. They could learn from their colleagues at ethnic and community-based museums, which have set the standard by establishing deep and meaningful civic involvement as their founding principle.

Civic engagement is invigorating. Museums that are fully and imaginatively engaged in community life have dynamic, risk-taking boards and staff leaders; committed staff who bring civic-minded values to museum work; and the ability to contend with ambiguity, reinvent conventional approaches, and learn from failure. There is a deeply internalized belief that community engagement matters; that the rationale for it does not need to be explained repeatedly; and that it should happen on many levels within the institution. The museum recognizes that the rewards of civic-mindedness are cumulative and long-term, and the outcomes, while not always measurable in conventional ways, can invigorate its purposes. The museum mines its assets to determine what it can bring to the table when it seeks complementary person-to-person and organization-to-organization relationships in the community. The museum's fiscal health reflects the community's strong endorsement; funding organizations respond positively to the museum because it is engaged with its community, and individuals willingly lend their support because of the museum's civic-minded mission and values. If such a museum is not already part of collaborative leadership for community change, then it is in a prime position to begin.

Learning civic engagement will require museums to commit to:
- *Examining and testing the beliefs and practices—institutional and individual —that shape their sense of civic purpose*

Transformation begins with deep inquiry into the museum's values, practices, and conventional approaches to fulfilling its mission. Individual board and staff members should reflect on their own views of civic-mindedness and how those beliefs affect their work.

- *Learning from promising models of community engagement and collaborative leadership*

Many museums need effective examples of experimentation, innovation, and change as well as workable mechanisms for sharing these stories. Community-based and ethnic museums, for example, provide models for other museums to emulate.

- *Nurturing staff growth and capability*

Museum professionals, trustees, and volunteers need more time and more opportunity for reflection on their work, study and dialogue with colleagues, and interaction with the community. A museum's civic possibilities are directly related to its board and staff's confidence in and enthusiasm for their own roles.

- *Replacing episodic partnerships with comprehensive, flexible, and sustained organization-to-organization relationships*

Museums should acknowledge and value the assets of community organizations so that together they can develop genuinely reciprocal and mutually accountable relationships—with more than the "usual suspects." Such relationships succeed only when they are integral to museums and community organizations instead of floating temporarily on the surface.

- *Expanding the museum's impact on the civic landscape*

More than venues for exhibitions and programs, museums should be more valued places at the heart of community life. Museums should explore more options for making themselves multidimensional gathering places where community comes alive.[3]

John Cotton Dana, founder of the Newark Museum, would not be surprised that museums are seeking a 21st-century definition of their civic purpose. In 1927, Dana wrote that "the best imaginings of museum enthusiasts have not yet set before us a clear picture of a museum of full and rich utility." [4] As one of the museum profession's most visionary thinkers, Dana knew that perceptions of "utility" would shift with the era and the context, and that museums would undergo corresponding—and never effortless—transformations.

Since the mid-1980s the American Association of Museums has led two major explorations of museums' purpose and posture in relation to their world. *Museums for a New Century* (1984) forecast societal trends and summed up the state of museums and the museum profession. The report recommended that museums seek greater impact as educational institutions, stronger collaboration among themselves and with other organizations, and heightened public understanding. *Museums for a New Century* had an internal focus, as museums sought a stronger self-definition and a firmer commitment to professional standards, but the project also represented AAM's first formal effort to include people from outside museums in the conversation.

Excellence and Equity: Education and the Public Dimension of Museums (1992) elaborated on an idea that *Museums for a New Century* had raised: the heightened potential of museums as places of learning. This report, which involved the profession in an active and sometimes fractious discussion, articulated principles of public service for museums and advocated seamless integration of the "public dimension" into every aspect of a museum's mission and operations. AAM's New Visions process, a framework for fostering internal change to support a public-oriented mission, arose from *Excellence and Equity*.

Another AAM project yielded significant findings about museums and communities. In the early 1990s, the Philadelphia Initiative for Cultural Pluralism supported programmatic partnerships between museums and community organizations and evaluated the results. The Philadelphia projects illuminated the challenges of museum-community relationships and the difficulty of mediating the intentions and needs of organizations with different missions and internal cultures. The publication *Museums in the Life of a City: Strategies for Community Partnerships* explained the factors that impede programmatic partnerships and the requisite steps to creating effective ones.

Museums & Community is grounded in AAM's earlier work but has taken a wholly different approach: listening to more than 700 people talk about the possibilities for museums as credible and effective agents for community vitality and change. AAM convened six dialogues between July 2000 and April 2001: in Providence, R.I.; Tampa, Fla.; Los Angeles; Detroit; Wichita, Kans.; and Bellingham, Wash. By design, about 65 percent of the participants represented diverse but elemental aspects of community life—people serving youth or seniors, involved with individuals on parole, leading faith-based communities, feeding and sheltering the homeless, serving in city government, managing libraries, delivering health care, developing low-income housing, running small businesses and grassroots nonprofits, creating art. The variety of people was impressive—and unprecedented for events initiated by the museum profession.

The dialogues engaged people who had not called upon museums or collaborated with them in the course of their work. These conversations explored the ease and difficulty of imagining the museum as a civic enterprise, considered creative alternatives for working together, and introduced people to the principles and potential of open dialogue.

Around the edges of the dialogues, AAM looked for indicators of the relationships—among organizations, among people—that must be at the heart of civic engagement and community building. Rather than define "community" for museums, the initiative sought an expansive concept of community engagement, which blurs the definitions of place and transcends the idea that focusing on "community" means targeting people of particular demographic characteristics.

Directly and indirectly, the dialogues considered some fundamental questions about museums' role in their communities:

• When we say that museums have potential as civic institutions that help build and sustain communities, what does that mean?

• What are museums' assets, and how can they be linked with those of other organizations?

• How can we combine the recognized intellectual strengths of museums—objects and knowledge—with their potential strengths as gathering places, safe and comforting places, places where people who differ can come together to consider tough issues?

- How can we replace one-sided programmatic collaborations with genuine partnerships based on mutual goals?

- How do we encourage museum professionals, trustees, and volunteers to engage with the community in open and useful ways, as civic leaders but also as community members?

These remain open questions that provide a new foundation for the next step in museums' evolution as places of, in Dana's words, "full and rich utility."

Considering the Context: Civil Society, Community Building, Social Capital

Since Sept. 11, 2001, the tremendous power of community has brought comfort, compassion, hope, and determination to Americans. Before this national tragedy, an active debate focused on the question, Are civic engagement and public-spiritedness alive and well, or are they in a troubling state of decline? There has been evidence to support both points of view, yet the response to the question may not matter as much as the attitudes and actions it inspires. A report by the Pew Partnership for Civic Change is more optimistic, finding that Americans feel deeply connected to their communities and to one another and are ready to work for change. Yet Robert Putnam, author of *Bowling Alone: The Collapse and Revival of American Community*, has seen a subtle but steady erosion of civic participation. However one portrays the state of civic engagement, or disengagement, there is general agreement that social capital—the relationships, associations, and networks that bind us together—is critical to healthy, invigorated communities.[5]

The social and economic issues that challenge communities are so complex that they require innovative, multidimensional solutions crafted by a broad spectrum of institutions and people working together. Collaborative leadership involves thinking and acting across boundaries, often among organizations that are unconventional partners. Communities are not well served when their needs and issues are carved into segments and assigned to particular institutions. Public safety, for example, is not just the responsibility of law enforcement and the courts; people also look out for each other. Collaborative leadership identifies the assets present in a community, brings those assets together in networks of relationships, and serves as the catalyst for creating new visions and solving problems.[6]

It relies on a foundation of trust and reciprocity, a good-faith belief that institutions working together will do so with honesty and mutual accountability.

Museums as Civic Enterprises

Museums are community institutions in the most basic of ways. They are established, familiar parts of the landscape. They contribute to the economy and to cultural tourism. They have strong connections to schools. They are places to meet friends, find shelter from hot weather, shop for a birthday gift, see a film or a performance, have a cup of coffee, or feed the spirit.

The Museums & Community dialogues asked participants to consider how museums could community institutions in other ways. Can they consciously build social capital? Can they create a strong, positive sense of place? Can they unite disparate parts of the community in constructive ways and build trust? Can they engage in the issues that influence or shape the community's health or well-being?

Emerging from the dialogues was an inventory of a museum's assets:

- *Accessible*: Available to a cross-section of people
- *Connected*: Inspires positive personal associations and a sense of ownership and identity
- *Safe*: A nonjudgmental place for expressing difficult or contentious ideas and beliefs
- *Objective*: Balanced, equitable, and open to multiple perspectives
- *Trustworthy*: Well-intentioned, credible, and with transparent motivation
- *Rewarding*: Emotionally engaging and intellectually stimulating
- *Substantive*: Confers value, provides context, and shapes meaning
- *Reciprocal*: Dedicated to shared goals and interests

Until now, museums have relied on two principal strategies for civic engagement: program-based relationships and audience development. Both approaches have helped museums establish community connections by finding common ground with organizations and people they may not have considered as partners, colleagues, visitors, or members. Program-based relationships have introduced diverse voices to exhibition and program development. Audience development efforts have helped museums segment their prospective audiences, identify underserved groups, and focus their resources on finely tuned, targeted programming.

Conversation during the dialogues revealed that although these strategies are community-oriented, they are not necessarily civic-minded. They do not always foster deep civic engagement. Working together or diversifying audiences is not enough. What is needed are reciprocal, co-created relationships that connect the assets and purposes of organizations. Otherwise, though there may be some residual value after the program has ended or the audience goals have been met, the museum and the community will not be ready to work together to support healthy community life. One-sided "collaborations" created wholly in service to the museum's mission or in response to funders' agendas, with inadequate attention to the missions of other participating organizations, leave the partner organizations feeling manipulated, exploited, and skeptical of the museum's motives. When audience development is the focal point and "community" is a code word for race, class, ethnicity, educational level, or other demographic characteristics, a museum's efforts can seem token and patronizing.

The dialogues uncovered other factors that challenge museums' capacity to learn and master civic engagement:

- Museums are limited by the public's perceptions that they control knowledge, expertise, and learning, that they are led and staffed by a homogenous group that floats above or passes through the community, and that they are not as "public" as libraries. These perceptions are mixed with enough reality to make them hard to dispel.

- Resistance from within museums is often disguised by references to mission. Instead of reviewing mission to ensure its relevance and vitality, some museums use the perceived limitations of mission as an excuse to avoid the kind of ongoing self-examination and change that connects a museum to its community

- The same assets that people respect are also liabilities. For example, museums' reputation for accuracy and authenticity inspires trust, but it also engenders doubt about their ability to reflect a variety of perspectives, especially when they are telling the stories of particular cultures.

- Museums' positive self-image as educational institutions is not fully endorsed by the community. Embedded in the image of educator is the attitude that, "we know and want to share," with the museum controlling knowledge, expertise, and learning. However, the public sees an institution that devalues their knowledge and what they, too, can teach.

Museums & Community looked outside the field for guidance in reimagining museums' civic role. The six dialogues reinforced the fact that there is challenging internal work to be done. Transformation of institutions begins within, with honest, thoughtful exploration of what the institution is about and, perhaps more important, conversations about the vision and values of people who work there. These questions may yield more, and more complex, questions instead of simple and direct answers, and they may provoke disagreement. But it is the process of inquiry—not the outcomes—that will lead a museum to redefine itself, increase its value, and find its way into the heart of the community.

As a starting point, the following questions could guide this process:

Attitudes

- What is the civic purpose of our museum?

- What are our questions, concerns, and conflicts surrounding civic engagement?

- What internal and external perceptions shape our museum's civic engagement?

- Is there internal resistance to civic engagement?

- What behavior—institutional and individual—promotes civic-minded values?

- What behavior stands in the way?

Practice

- Can the governing board legitimately claim to represent the community, and would the community agree?

- Does the museum engage in exclusive practices in any of its operations, including hiring, contracting, and purchasing?

- How should the qualifications of those who work our museum change?

- Should trustees and professionals understand community dynamics as a prerequisite for board service and for employment?

- Should museum professionals view themselves as citizens first and museum staff second?

- What can our museum do to encourage staff to be engaged with the community?

- Do we have the capacity to stimulate systemic change, both within our museum and in the community?

Ownership, Access, and Trust
- Whose viewpoints and voices shape the museum's purpose and programs?
- What is the balance between a museum's authority and the community's desire to develop some aspect of the stories told through exhibitions?
- Does shared authority imply that the museum no longer controls meanings and interpretations?
- Can we think of ourselves as collections of community assets? What are those assets?
- Can we invite the community to help identify assets? Can we work with the community to make best use of those assets?

Relationships
- What are our motivations for relationships in the community?
- What are our skills at developing programmatic relationships?
- What are our skills at developing organization-to-organization relationships?
- If our skills are limited, how will we improve them?

No two museums will go about this process of inquiry in the same way. It is a lengthy, time-consuming process that honors the museum field in all its variety, but recognizes the need to broaden its horizons. Mission, size, history, type of museum, community context, and numerous other factors will affect the design and degree of the dialogue. But whatever the shape of the process, it is an essential one. It could make the difference between a museum with purpose and impact and one that exists on the margins of community life—an object of great public affection, but with a weak and ineffectual voice in the community.

AAM's Commitment to the Inquiry

Museums need guideposts, encouragement, and the capacity to create tools that work for them as they learn and master the process of civic engagement. Many museums and museum professionals are already working to reshape and reinvent their civic purposes. To support this inquiry into civic role, the AAM Board of Directors has pledged its leadership to:

- Strengthen and develop relationships with other national organizations involved in the quest for community and civil society

- Support and develop successful museum strategies for pursuing an expanded civic role

- Support and develop museum professionals' understanding of their own civic roles

- Encourage funders and public policy makers that support museums in the process of learning and mastering civic engagement

For AAM, as for museums, the pursuit of civic engagement is a process of questioning and learning that must penetrate the organization and inform its work. The goal is to begin a deeper exploration of the possibilities for museums as civic enterprises and to urge museums to create and share inventive models.

True and meaningful transformation occurs when people and organizations reframe the way they think about the world—their own internal world and the world around them. For museums, the times demand inquiry and action—subtle and overt, deceptively simple and extraordinarily complex— that will lead to "full and rich utility" and a mastery of the critical work of civic engagement.

Notes

1. For a range of perspectives on civil society and community building, see *Community Works: The Revival of Civil Society in America*, edited by E. J. Dionne, Jr. (Washington, D.C.: Brookings Institution Press, 1998).

2. A national survey commissioned by the American Association of Museums and released in 2001 documents this high level of trust. Almost nine out of 10 Americans (87 percent) find museums to be trustworthy, including 38 percent who see museums as one of the most trusted sources.

3. Ray Oldenburg describes "third places" as places where "community is most alive and people are most themselves." They "exist on neutral ground and serve to level their guests to a condition of social equality." Oldenburg, *The Great Good Place: Cafés, Coffee Shops, Bookstores, Bars, Hair Salons and Other Hangouts in the Heart of a Community* (New York: Marlowe & Co., 1989), pp. 14–19.

4. Dana, "Should Museums Be Useful?" (1927), in *The New Museum: Selected Writings by John Cotton Dana*, edited by William A. Peniston (Washington, D.C.: AAM and Newark Museum, 1999), p. 133.

5. Robert D. Putnam, *Bowling Alone: The Collapse and Revival of American Community* (New York: Simon and Schuster, 2000); *Better Together: Report of the Saguaro Seminar on Civic Engagement in America* (Cambridge, Mass.: John F. Kennedy School of Government, Harvard University, 2000), available online from www.bettertogether.org; Pew Partnership for Civic Change, *Ready, Willing, and Able: Citizens Working for Change* (Charlottesville, Va.: Pew Partnership, 2001).

6. The Web site of the Pew Partnership for Civic Change, a project of the Pew Charitable Trusts, describes the attributes, skills, and "roadmarkers" of collaborative leadership: www.pew-partnership.org.

Ellen Hirzy is the consulting writer for AAM's Museums & Community Initiative.

A Framework for Civic Engagement

THE CIVIC LANDSCAPE
. . . .

By Christopher T. Gates

In the aftermath of the tragic events of Sept. 11, 2001, institutions of all kinds—public, private, and nonprofit—must reexamine the role they play in the broad processes of strengthening democracy, encouraging civic engagement, and building better communities. It is no longer enough for each of us to exist and work in our separate silos, doing "our" work and leaving the public agenda to others. We must find ways to transform the concept of public purpose, the definition of the public good, and the determination of the public agenda.

In old civics books, the division of societal responsibilities was clearly laid out. It was the private sector's job to create jobs and wealth. It was the public sector's job to identify the public agenda and provide for the public good. And it was the nonprofit sector's job to encourage and direct volunteerism and philanthropy. The implications of this model for citizenship were equally clear. It became the citizens' job to vote once every two years and, in that way, turn over the responsibility for making things better to those working in the public sector. That is the traditional definition of what people call representative democracy, where leaders are elected to represent the will of the people, allowing citizens to trust that those leaders would solve society's problems.

Yet one can make the case that this was not how the framers of our republic intended our society and political system to function. Citizenship was never intended to be as passive as it has become in this country over the past several decades. In *Democracy in America*, Alexis de Tocqueville described what he found in this country over the nine months he spent traveling here in 1831-1832. He was particularly struck by what he referred to as America's "associational life," writing, "Americans of all ages, all conditions, and all dispositions, constantly form associations . . . religious, moral, serious, futile, general or restricted, enormous or diminutive . . . to give entertainments, to found seminaries, to build inns, to construct churches, to diffuse books, to send missionaries. . . ." Our nation was founded out of a fundamental concern that government could become too powerful. De Tocqueville noted our efforts both to limit the absolute power of government and to have a more direct part in the governing and problem-solving process.

Although today we are more likely to call these activities "community building," the passion for forming associations lives on within the American spirit. The National Civic League (NCL), for example, has been building community for over a century. NCL was founded in 1894 by turn-of-the-century reformers, including a young Teddy Roosevelt and Louis Brandeis, and its staff have been writing about and studying the concepts of good government, citizenship, and community since that time. Roosevelt made the case for practicing what he called "self government" in America's communities. His theory was that our communities could only reach their potential when all citizens, no matter their background, recognized that they had a role to play in making things better. He also clearly was cautioning against a model of representative democracy that went too far, where citizens would lose sight of the active role they were intended to play.

NCL became one of the organizations that helped drive several decades of reform in our political and governmental institutions. This Good Government movement focused largely on corruption, particularly among elected officials. In the late 19th century, many of our communities were run by political bosses and political machines that made high art of rewarding supporters and punishing opponents. Reformers felt that the health of our communities and our democracy were being threatened and sought to transform the way politics was practiced, how government interacted with citizens, and the methods government used to fulfill its public purpose.

One hundred years later, the challenges faced by those in the field of community building might seem quite different. Gone, for the most part, are political bosses and machines. More often than not, government is efficient, professional, entrepreneurial, and fair. Services are provided to all, not just those who supported the few in power. And while some may continue to question the effects of the Florida vote on the 2000 presidential election, those events were even more remarkable because of their uniqueness. People were not used to seeing our electoral process break down.

But one might be able to make the case that the core issues being faced by community builders have only changed in shape and form, not content. One hundred years ago, the media fed the deep cynicism of the public; the same is true today. One hundred years ago, citizens felt that the political process did not reflect their voices or concerns; the current debate over such issues as campaign finance reform seems to arise from the same concern. One hundred years ago, people questioned whether government could meet the needs of their communities. Despite a positive shift in the months after Sept. 11, that lack of faith in government programs largely remains. One hundred years ago, citizens felt they needed to create new institutions to solve the problems. Today, the tone, tenor, scope and scale of our problems are different, but our challenges are frustratingly similar to those faced by civic reformers a century ago.

In his book *Bowling Alone: The Collapse and Revival of American Community*, Robert Putnam points out that 100 years ago this nation had experienced changes in every aspect of life, including shifts in living patterns from rural to urban and in employment from agricultural to industrial and a massive wave of immigration. These changes reduced the connections between people, made old forms of collective problem-solving obsolete, and forced the country to invent new ways of building what Putnam calls bridging and bonding social capital—i.e., developing relationships of trust and reciprocity both with those who are like us (bonding) and with those who are different from us (bridging). As a result of these shifts, there was a burst of civic invention and activity that dramatically enlarged and reinvented the associational life that de Tocqueville had referred to 60 years earlier. As the good government activists were cleaning up the practice of politics and the business of government, other reformers were busy creating institutions such as the Salvation Army (1880), Red Cross (1881), Knights of Columbus (1882), Sierra Club (1892), Volunteers of America (1896), 4-H (1901), Goodwill Industries (1902), Big Brothers (1903), Rotary (1905), Big Sisters (1908), Community Chest/United Way (1913), Lions Clubs (1917), and the League of Women Voters (1920). At the same time, activists also were seeking to reform the cultural arena. For example, the American Association for State and Local History was formed in 1904, AAM in 1906, and the College Art Association in 1911.

One hundred years later we are again facing significant and fundamental shifts in the way our society and our economy function. Our society is far more diverse, urbanization has intensified significantly, and the economic base has shifted from industrial to technological, as reflected by the internal operations of many of our industries. Changing employment patterns—along with the cynicism that has is so fashionable these days—have affected significantly the time that people are willing and able to spend on formal and informal associational life. In *Bowling Alone*, Putnam documents at length the decline in such activities as volunteering, attending meetings, joining clubs, playing cards, and even having dinner with family or friends.

But, according to Putnam and others, this moment of economic and societal transition provides an opportunity to reinvigorate our traditional forms of social and political engagement and invent new forms that may be more appropriate for our times. One of the new approaches to building stronger communities is the Healthy Communities movement, embraced by the World Health Organization several decades ago but only introduced in the United States in the mid-1980s. The theory behind Healthy Communities is that too much attention is focused on "sick care"; that our societies have become places where people are well served once they become sick, ill, or in need, but we have stopped looking for ways to ensure that people stayed healthy in the first place. The movement argued that we must invest some of our resources in activities that will reduce the demand for health care in our communities. The Western European planners who first embraced this theory pointed out that ambulance runs, hospital stays, and extended illnesses directly correlated to unemployment, under-employment, and a lack of education and meaningful community-based cultural opportunities. In other words, investing in literacy programs, job-training programs, community centers, and ball fields can only improve the health of our communities and their citizens.

The midnight basketball leagues that became so popular in the United States two decades ago are a real and specific example of this theory at work. Before the leagues were formed, police and ambulance drivers in urban areas could almost predict when and where they would be called. Without safe spaces and supervised activities, young people would invariably behave in ways that would lead to calls to the 911 operator. As a result, all over the country, police departments and neighborhood activists began organizing midnight basketball leagues to provide young people with a safe, supervised haven. Rather than wait for people to ask for help, these activists —spending a fraction of the resources that would have been used on healthcare—worked to improve personal health and build community.

This cultural aspect of the Healthy Communities theory reinforces Putnam's idea about social capital. According to Putnam, when we have higher levels of bonding and bridging social capital, we are not only better off as a society, we are better off as individuals. That connection to community is not some kind of altruistic, utopian good, but something that improves the quality of life in our communities and our own levels of personal health. "The more integrated we are with our community, the less likely we are to experience colds, heart attacks, strokes, cancer, depression, and premature death of all sorts," Putnam writes in *Bowling Alone*. "Such protective effects have been confirmed for close family ties, for friendship networks, for participation in social events, and even for simple affiliation with religious and other civic associations."

If social connectedness is integral to our form of government and good for us as individuals, as communities, and as a society, what is the role of museums in this effort? Given the range of activities museums undertake it is clear that they play a vital part in increasing and enhancing social connectedness. Anything that museums do to celebrate the unique cultures of a community affects it. Anything that museums do to attract a diverse audience of citizens to their programs helps build it. And anything museums do to create interactive experiences that people can share and discuss enriches it.

Let us examine how museums affect the three processes mentioned at the beginning of this article—strengthening democracy, encouraging civic engagement, and building communities. Obviously these objectives are not the direct focus of museum programs, but the values that museums encourage are relevant to these goals. Promoting these three processes requires a high level of trust throughout society, and trust is, of course, a function of social connectedness. As Putnam says, trust can be fostered within groups on the basis of bonding social capital, and it can be fostered between groups on the basis of bridging social capital. But modern societies are too complex and diverse to thrive on bonding social capital alone, and the human need for solidarity cannot be satisfied solely by bridging social capital. Museums are at the nexus of these two types of human interaction.

Museums are vital institutions for preserving memory, sustaining culture, and creating identity. This trinity—memory, culture, and identity—is essential to the moral and psychological development of individuals, communities, and societies. These three factors deeply influence the character and values of a community and its members and determine which qualities of citizenship find root and flourish. Part of how we make sense of our lives is by learning and telling stories about who we are, where we come from, and where we are going. Even in this postmodern period, "meaning making" depends heavily on narration. By providing the means to preserve memory, sustain culture, and create identity, museums help equip us to understand each other and ourselves. And it is this understanding that animates our efforts to strengthen democracy, promote civic engagement, and build community.

Consider some recent historical examples in which different societies sought to suppress the cultural freedoms museums help encourage. It is no accident that in addition to curtailing political freedom, the rulers of closed and repressive societies limit cultural autonomy and seek to control how the past is viewed. In fact, the more repressive the society, the more apparent these practices are. In addition to the various atrocities committed by each state, Nazi Germany attacked what it regarded as degenerate art, Stalinist Russia imposed a chilling censorship on the arts, and Maoist China underwent a ruthless cultural revolution. In our more recent history, we saw the Taliban forbid music and destroy Buddhist statues in Afghanistan. It is significant that all four regimes were threatened by free creative expression.

Museums play an important role in validating both the unique stories of diverse cultures and the shared story that unites all the members of a society. These are the bonding and bridging functions that museums contribute to a society's store of social capital. Clearly, different museums will build social capital in different ways, and some will be better at producing bonding than bridging social capital and vice versa. While the focus of any particular museum will influence the kind of social capital that is fostered, it also will define, in large measure, the museum's community. People may be more inclined to see each city's art, history, and science museums as belonging to very different communities. But though this perception helps museums sustain a geographically dispersed community of people interested in the arts or history or science, museums are located in discrete physical spaces and contribute to communities of place as well. In this capacity, museums play a bridging role by connecting residents to the wider cultural and intellectual worlds represented within their walls.

Christopher T. Gates is president of the National Civic League, Denver (www.ncl.org), a nonprofit, nonpartisan organization dedicated to strengthening citizen democracy by transforming democratic institutions.

COMING TO THE CENTER OF COMMUNITY LIFE

By Maria-Rosario Jackson

In any community, a museum is a special place. It holds treasures, marvels, and stories—old and new. A museum has the authority and responsibility to highlight objects and ideas that compel, challenge, inspire, and move people to be more reflective, critical, and humane. But all too frequently, museums are considered merely sources of childhood memories, places to take out-of-town visitors, or institutions that are elitist, inaccessible, detached, or irrelevant. Too often, they are on the sidelines of civic life. Through its Museums & Community Initiative (M&C), AAM has given the museum field a noble challenge—to stretch its boundaries, step away from the sidelines, come to the center of civic life, and become a more active participant and even a leader in social-capital and community-building processes.

At a time when people and institutions are struggling to make sense of a world that is changing rapidly and dramatically—a world that is constantly being destroyed, reinvented, and rebuilt—people are asking how they fit in and how they can matter. In this context, AAM's challenge to museums— *Step up. Come to the center. Join in. Take responsibility. We need to build community.*—is exactly right. But what does that mean, really? To what are museums being asked to contribute? How can they contribute? And what do they have to offer? No one organization, institution, or individual can build community on its own. Building community involves creating and strengthening social bonds that make possible broad-based collective action in support of a common good. That requires diverse groups of people, organizations, and institutions to work together and bring to the table what they have and what is needed at a given time. In any community, a museum is but a piece of a puzzle, a part of the solution.

Within the museum field, there are excellent examples of institutions, often ethnic and community-based museums, that from their founding have worked at the core of community life. This essay is directed not at them but at those museums that have not operated as community institutions in the past. It is based on years of research on community development, community building, and social change strategies around the country, as well as the roles of artists, arts and cultural organizations, and various kinds of cultural engagement in building community.

Coming to the Center: Making Sense of Chaos

The M&C dialogues were an important first step that allowed participants to interact with other civic actors, explore possible roles of a museum in the abstract, and make known museums' intent to participate in community-building processes. However, as museums prepare to become more active and committed participants in civic dialogues and action (ongoing and new), we must have more clarity about what their contributions might be.

It would be so easy if the best path to the center of building community was clearly marked. If only every community had a single, clearly articulated vision with corresponding plans and goals that its citizens and institutions could pursue wholeheartedly. Things would be so much easier if there were a place where anyone interested in building community could get a description of all of the various players as well as information about what they have to offer.

But the reality is messier and more complicated. People in community-based organizations—such as schools, hospitals, and museums—have the sense that they are working for the collective good, contributing to a process that will make the community whole and healthy. However, often the work of individual organizations, admirable and well-intended as it may be, is not connected to a coherent vision or plan that encourages optimal and strategic contributions. The chamber of commerce may have a vision, but the city council will have another, and the cultural affairs division, yet another. The same is true of community-development corporations, social service organizations, and ad hoc coalitions and committees. Some plans are explicit and coherent; others are not. Some are citywide, while others are neighborhood or population specific. Some are short term; others long term. Some planning documents and vision statements are the result of in-depth community planning processes from the bottom up; others are the result of top-down management. Many plans have been shelved and forgotten. Others have been implemented in fits and starts. Still, an understanding of these community visions and individual initiatives is essential for the museum professional seeking to bring his institution to the center of civic life. These documents and processes bring into focus key community actors, priorities, and aspirations from various perspectives.

Gaining a comprehensive understanding of community concerns and efforts to address them requires doing some on-the-ground research—delving into the worlds of city government, social service organizations, community-development corporations, ad hoc civic committees, and other types of agencies to find out about recent and current initiatives focused on improving quality of life. This work involves assembling various community vision statements and plans and observing ongoing community-planning initiatives (both bottom-up and top-down efforts), and then reviewing the information collected with the following questions in mind:

• What are the community's greatest concerns?

• What are its greatest assets?

• When were plans or initiatives created?

• Who was involved in creating them?

• Was it a top-down or bottom-up effort?

• Have the plans been implemented and the initiatives completed? How or why not?

• What are the dynamics and politics of the meetings observed?

• Which resources and perspectives are present?

• Which resources and perspectives are missing?

• Does the museum have a presence in the formulation of community problems or solutions?

With a bird's eye view of the community's initiatives, an understanding of community priorities, and an awareness of the key actors, the museum professional will be better equipped to assess how his institution (and its staff) can effectively engage in contemporary community processes. Armed with new information and insights, the institution can ask itself if and how the community's current and future plans intersect with the values and orientations of the museum. Can the museum bolster ongoing efforts by working within existing structures, such as committees and working groups? Or should the museum launch a new initiative that connects to the community's ongoing work? Who are the museum's most strategic collaborators? And if community-building practitioners seldom think of museum professionals as colleagues in the process, how can museums position themselves as resources and potential collaborators?

Collaboration

Collaboration is a crucial aspect of the AAM challenge to the museum field. Often, this will mean building relationships with individuals and organizations that are very different from museums' traditional partners, particularly if the museum aims to become more inclusive, diverse, and relevant.

A collaboration can take many forms; there is no "right" structure. At their best, collaborations facilitate the work at hand, change to accommodate the particular circumstances of the participants, have a purpose, and involve relationships that enable the achievement of individual and collective goals. They require organizational flexibility, time, patience, staff, resources, and (sometimes) mediation; this is especially true of long-term efforts between dissimilar players.

Collaborations can be imposed or organic—an arranged (sometimes shotgun) marriage orchestrated by some outside force, or a relationship rooted in mutually recognized strengths and needs. They can be formal or informal—based on specific organizational roles spelled out in a memorandum of understanding, or only on personal contacts and verbal interactions. They can be short or long term. A group of organizations may come together to produce a one-time event, or they may rely on each other year after year to create something that both satisfies community expectations and is central to each partner's mission. Collaborations can be reactive or proactive. They can be formed in response to crisis, or they may arise out of a shared vision for the future.

People committed to collaboration must remain open to the possible range of configurations and paths that will lead to shared goals. Organic collaboration that grows out of mutual resources and needs is often the ideal. However, imposed collaborations can be useful if the rationale for bringing the organizations together is on target and the partners see mutual benefit in the relationship. Some collaborations start out informally and eventually establish a formal structure; others remain informal and work just fine. In some cases, a memorandum of understanding is essential to solidifying institutional commitment and keeping collaboration going. In other cases, it may just get in the way, stifle creativity, and create unnecessary barriers.

A short-term collaboration may be exactly what is needed for a one-time effort with a clear beginning and end. Why burden organizations with sustaining a structure for collaboration that no longer serves a purpose? Celebrate the accomplishment and move on. Hopefully, that short-term experience will be the basis for a future collaboration. On the other hand, if organizations need to rely on each other continuously, be explicit about that need and create the climate and structures that make ongoing joint work possible. In addition, while the collaboration may have started as a reaction to crisis, that initial experience may be the basis for future collaborations that are proactive in nature.

The most fruitful collaborations are based on mutually recognized strengths and needs and take the form and intensity that best facilitates the work. This is especially important in cases where the organizations have distinct organizational cultures and different (and seemingly incompatible) standards for success and excellence.

In my own research I have followed the efforts of large cultural institutions, small community-based arts organizations, community-development corporations, social service organizations, and churches committed to working together on various art-based community-building initiatives. Over time, these organizations have sought to reconcile differences in language, technological capacity, bureaucratic processes, evaluation, and documentation standards and practices, as well as differences in opinion about how the projects should grow and change, given growing and changing organizational goals.

In one case, a community-development corporation, social service organization, community arts organization, and large cultural institution offered free art-making workshops in preparation for various neighborhood festivals. Early in the effort there were language conflicts and misunderstandings about professional and organizational priorities and standards. Joint debriefing sessions and openness among staff and leaders from the various agencies were the key to allaying tensions. For example, the director of the social service agency could not understand why an artist running a workshop was annoyed because he didn't receive the exact art materials he had requested. To her, the materials seemed fine; she was more concerned about the 50 kids waiting to start the delayed workshop. The artist also was concerned about the kids, but in a different way. He felt that without the appropriate materials he could not do his job well. In a joint debriefing session, the artist and the director discussed their experience and, as a result, each became more sensitive to the other's needs and expectations. The experience turned out to be an important building block for future work.

At one festival where workshop participation far exceeded expectations, some partners were happy that word was getting out about the terrific opportunities being offered. Others worried that the high demand for the workshops would spill over into other programs that were already at capacity. Still others were concerned that the events would lose their intimacy, the neighborhood/community feel, an important aspect of the program they wanted to nurture and protect. In addition, the smaller organizations were frequently frustrated with the bureaucratic processes in the large institutions that resulted in lags between disbursements of resources. That was a burden for small organizations on tight budgets that had difficulty fronting money for the programs.

There are many tensions involved in collaborations, particularly those over the long term. But with time, patience, commitment, and (internal or external) mediation, the chasm can close or at least become smaller. People involved in the collaboration learn a new language; come to understand the priorities, practices, and resources of others; and in the process invent their own collective nomenclature, practices, and standards of success. Still, there are considerable obstacles to achieving an optimal outcome. New nomenclature, practices, and hybrid measures of success may be at odds with standard methods of evaluation in certain fields. In fact, sometimes the entities (such as public and private funders) to which collaborating organizations are accountable will not subscribe to these new hybrid measures. Moreover, collaborations that rely in large part on committed individuals are at risk when those individuals leave organizations or become distracted by other duties.

If an institution is committed to collaboration, it must develop the institutional capacity to create and sustain many different kinds of relationships.

And the leadership must be committed to nourishing those relationships. After obtaining a better sense of how it can contribute to community-building processes, a museum should consider the following.

- Is the institution able to create contexts in which strategic, fruitful—seemingly unlikely—collaborations can form?

- Are there staff dedicated to identifying opportunities for collaboration and nurturing those relationships to fruition?

- Can collaboration with a wide range of organizations in other fields (i.e., community development, social services, etc.) become part of the museum's work culture?

- What skills does collaboration across fields require?

- Are the museum's leaders and staff sufficiently versatile, diverse, and culturally competent (on professional, racial/ethnic, and other fronts) to engage with networks already involved in building community?

- What can the museums bring to the collaboration?

- Can the museum staff and leaders reassess what they have to offer in light of ongoing community pursuits?

- Can they present those assets in terms that people outside the museum field can understand?

What Can a Museum Offer?

The M&C dialogues identified a number of museum assets: expertise and knowledge (of various sorts), staff, employment opportunities, collections, exhibits, and space, among others. The dialogues helped the participating museums to consider more deeply their potential contributions to community-building processes and to realize that the determination of whether something is an asset is subjective. Given the community's priorities, existing assets, needs, and perceptions of the museum, how should an institution reassess its possible contributions? In some cases, museums will have valuable resources that meet a current need. In others, museums will have to create a context for their offerings, modify existing assets, and/or invent new ones.

Take this hypothetical example. A museum has committed to become a more active participant in local community-building processes. The museum leaders and staff have done their research and have identified a community-planning initiative they want to support. They see that the organizing committee is unable to find an appropriate site for an important meeting intended to attract a broad cross-section of citizens. The museum is centrally located and has space that is available; in good faith, it offers the space for the meeting.

If the invitees to the meeting perceive the museum as a serious, neutral, and accessible institution, the museum has made an important and significant contribution to the community-building process. In fact, affiliation with the museum may even give the community's initiative more stature and credibility. However, if the museum has been viewed in the past as elitist and exclusive, how will its offer be perceived by the community? What does the space represent? Will the invitees feel comfortable? Will they show up at all? If the museum has a public image problem, perhaps it should take incremental steps to engage its underserved constituents before it can be the host it seeks to be. For instance, it might decide to diversify its leadership and staff, ramp up its outreach efforts, modify its programming, or cohost the event with an organization that has broad-based credibility.

A museum seeking to contribute to community-building processes is not limited to its current inventory of assets. On the contrary, the field and the community should re-evaluate museum assets and, in fact, create new ones. Museums also can incorporate more community priorities in their exhibits and special events. Of course, there is no need to tailor all museum programming to community-improvement initiatives. But institutions can refocus some of their offerings and be creative and entrepreneurial about making new connections between museum commitments and community concerns. A museum's renewed dedication to engagement in community life can lead to imaginative, rich, and relevant programs as well as introduce a host of new stakeholders to the institution.

Conclusion

As museums seek to clarify their roles at the center of civic life, approach collaborative efforts with dissimilar organizations, and reassess what they have to offer, important questions remain. What is the community's role in reaching out to museums? What assets can museums, social service agencies, community-development corporations, other social-change-focused enterprises, and citizens share with each other? Materials for new collections? Ideas for new programs? Better strategies for community outreach? Leadership?

If museums are to be supported in this undertaking, how will their contributions be documented, evaluated, and rewarded inside and outside the field? Do museums' current systems of validation reward, hamper, or penalize this new orientation? How can institutions that train current and future museum professionals integrate this kind of work into their courses? How can the experiences and expertise of ethnic and community-based institutions, which already have strong community connections, be harvested and made available to the field?

AAM's challenge to museums to engage in civic processes and play an important role in building community is no small request. It requires museums and other organizations to stretch their boundaries, take on new themes, and work with individuals and organizations that may be alien to them. This can be difficult, frustrating, and time and resource intensive. But the prospect of a more engaged and relevant museum holds much promise. In the long run, museums will benefit in many ways, as will the communities that they seek to serve and inspire.

Resources

Jackson, Maria-Rosario, and Peter Marris, "Comprehensive Community Initiatives: Overview of an Emerging Community Improvement Orientation," paper presented at Urban Institute Community Building Seminar Series, 1996, pp. 27-30.

Maria-Rosario Jackson is a senior research associate and director of the Urban Institute's Arts, Culture, and Communities Program, Washington, D.C.

THE LENS OF ORGANIZATIONAL CULTURE

By Daniel Kertzner

An interesting shift is taking place in museums across the country. The traditional, internally focused conversations about "audience building" and "outreach" are giving way to discussions about how the museum can build and sustain community relationships and place itself at the heart of its community. In response to a variety of modern crises—crime, racial and ethnic conflicts, rising high-school drop-out rates, and the erosion of neighborhood life, etc.—museums are realizing that they have assets that both can make communities stronger and help those communities build the capacity to solve their own problems. Today's museum professionals are seeking strategies that can help them become better citizens. They are asking, individually and collectively, how can we understand what institutional and individual museum-community engagement looks like?

The study of organizational culture—the living, dynamic interplay between the shared beliefs, values, norms, and practices that operate, consciously and un-consciously, in an organization—can provide a useful lens for exploring the relationships between museums and other organizations and museum staff and community members at the heart of civic engagement. Museums can gain valuable insights into how they function internally and externally and relate to others in the community. This is a particularly useful undertaking for institutions that already have begun to explore a potentially expanded civic role within their communities and for museum professionals who seek to identify their personal civic mission.

According to Edgar Schein, one of the pre-eminent experts in the field of organizational change management and human dynamics, culture is "a basic pattern of assumptions invented, discovered, or developed by a given group as it learns to cope with its problems of external adaptation and internal integration." Those assumptions, he notes, are taught to new members of the group as "the correct way to perceive, think, and relate to those problems."[1] Schein calls the process an organization uses to define and learn how to survive in its environment—i.e., determining the mission, strategies, goals, structures, practices, evaluation, and solutions—"external adaptation." If issues relating to external adaptation comprise the skeleton of an organization's culture, then issues of internal integration provide the "meat on the bones." Internal integration, says Schein, is the process of creating and maintaining relationships among a set of individuals who are doing something together. Several things can affect the development of those relationships, including differences in language and conceptual categories; group boundaries and criteria for inclusion and exclusion; and ideas about power, status, peer relationships, and what overarching ideals drive actions within the organization.

Institutional responses to external adaptation and internal integration correspond to what Karl Weick, professor of organizational behavior and psychology at the University of Michigan Business School, calls the "organizing processes" from which a sense of the institution unfolds. Once they are part of the organizational culture, these responses give rise to the basic assumptions and values of an organization.

This essay examines the culture of three organizations involved in arts-based civic dialogue programming. The Everett Dance Theatre, Providence, R.I., is a professional dance theatre with a strong community focus, dedicated to developing young artists and providing them with steady employment. The mission of the Massachusetts-based Cambridge Multicultural Arts Center is to present quality programs that use the arts to combat racism and bigotry. The Washington (D.C.) Performing Arts Society aims to increase the opportunity for artists and the public to share the performing arts.

The missions, histories, and tasks of these organizations obviously differ from those of museums. However, the processes they used to become catalysts in their communities—and establish both relationships with the wider community and the internal practices to support those relationships—can help museums transform into civic enterprises.

Several factors relating to organizational culture will influence the museum's relationship to its community; some of them are discussed below, in no particular order.

Power and Status

Museums seeking to transform themselves into more civically engaged institutions must take issues of power and status into account. Community relationships often fail because one partner feels shortchanged or abused. Museums partnering with community organizations may appear to have far more significant resources: more money and staff, larger facilities, etc. But they must understand that community organizations also have significant assets: a deep knowledge of their communities and constituencies, the capacity to seek nontraditional outcomes, experience with community building, etc. Museums have to resist the impulse to dictate the agenda, and ensure that all questions relating to attitude, approach, ownership, access, and trust are resolved to everyone's satisfaction. For example, staff at the Washington Performing Arts Society realized that if they did not deal with the power differentials and inequities inherent in their community relationships, the collaborations would fail. The society's response (see "Sharing Authority," below) greatly influenced its subsequent relationships with other organizations.

Negotiating differences in power and status is a subtle and complex process. It involves navigating a world of personal and group histories and many different kinds of identities. It involves the personal and the political, the private and the civic. This clash of histories, ideas, and perceptions can derail even the best-intentioned museum attempts to become civic enterprises. By utilizing a distinct set of skills, partnering organizations can successfully work through differences in power and status.

Sharing Authority

Simultaneously engaging and sharing authority with community participants is the best strategy for resolving the power dynamics involved in community work. The way the Washington Performing Arts Society communicates with its community is at the core of its community-related success. The staff works closely with the community, developing and building appropriate relationships and programming. In this regard, the society does not impose its agenda on others, but complements the efforts of organizations already in the process of building a constituency.

The society's Gospel Showcase provides a good example of an arts organization working to fill a community need. As they were developing the showcase, the staff recognized the society could not unilaterally impose its own agenda. "We had to overcome the temptation to perform at people [rather than engage] people in the artistic development," says Vice President and General Manager Bill Reeder. "We were spending most of our time trying to convince someone that our set of values is the dominant set. What we actually denied [people was] the invitation to contribute to our work." By talking with community members, the staff discovered that gospel was alive and well in the community and that concerts were a regular occurrence. They also determined that a large choir, which was beyond the capacity of any one church or organization to set up, would provide an outlet for creative expression that was desired by community. Thus the society was able to engage the community as a facilitator and convener, a role museums also are well positioned to play.

Communication

Good communication, so essential for resolving power and status dynamics, requires organizations to commit to being transparent about their motivations and assumptions. The Washington Performing Arts Society's efforts to build relationships with its community partners brought into play larger issues of societal inequality. The society resolved these differences by being up-front about them and emphasizing honest dialogue, even when it was difficult. At the start of a new project, the society and its community collaborators publicly state the resources each can bring to the table. According to Kim Chan, director of programming, "the sharing of human and economic resources has to be a part of it. And if it's not, then that's grounds for dismantling the project. There are power dynamics when [you engage] with the community. People have to be willing to admit that and that makes people really uncomfortable."

In their 1996 report *Beyond Stabilization: Arts Funding and Organizational Development*, Richard Evans and Laurel Jones highlight the importance of an organization's capacity to operate in a state of uncertainty and discomfort. They describe the health of an organization in terms of its ability "to sustain a 'creative tension' between a compelling vision and its current circumstances."[2] Such creative tension often encourages an organization to take actions aligned with both the long term (even when it is uncomfortable) and the short term.

Common Language and Conceptual Framework

Museums must understand that their new partners in the community are not likely to share the same vocabulary. They must not let this limit them. As Therese Jungels, company administrator at the Everett Dance Theatre, says, "In order to be effective in communities, you have to know communities." Part of that process is finding a common language and frame of reference for working together. As the dance company began to develop a deeper relationship with the community, it made sure that its work and performances resonated with the community, and that staff and the community understood and spoke a shared language.

But finding that common language can be an obstacle to a museum's goal to become a civic enterprise. As museums seek to function as part of a network of community relationships, it becomes hard to navigate the different histories and values—which play a significant role in shaping individual and organizational perception—that people and organizations bring to any project. Yet if museums are to build and sustain community, they will have to learn to move the conversation beyond individual concerns and issues in a way that still deals with the complexities of each situation. This approach will engender credibility and trust among all parties and allow museums to help orchestrate a public conversation that accommodates individual and group concerns.

Inclusion/Exclusion

To be at the center of community life, museums must be welcoming places for all of the community. For many institutions, that means repositioning their current relationship with the community. The Everett Dance Theatre, for example, succeeds as a community institution because it has always placed a premium on inclusion. Says Artistic Director Dorothy Jungels: "Whoever was in the company . . . dictated what it became. . . . Everyone could be a part of [the dance]." In a Feb. 20, 1996, *Village Voice* review of a dance piece titled *Body of Work*, Deborah Jowitt wrote: "I loved the way Jungels and her engaging regular performers-collaborators, Walter Ferrero,

Aaron Jungels, Rachel Jungels, and Marvin Novogrodski, integrated three young people into the project without making any distinctions based on age or experience."[3]

Individual staff also can strive to be inclusive in their interactions with community. Performance artist Marty Pottenger saw the importance of inclusivity as she created a public art project in New York in response to the events of Sept. 11, 2001. "I began to understand the critical need for people to stick together, listen to each other, and to both stand up for what is right and not cut people out of the circle of community," she writes.[4] Arts-based civic dialogue and collaborative efforts on issues of public concern require a commitment to listening to multiple points of view.[5] For museums, inviting the community inside may take many forms, including a willingness to listen to a community's many stories.

For the Washington Performing Arts Society, issues of inclusion are highlighted by the its relationship to artists. According to Kim Chan, the society stopped thinking of "artists as the product that you bought and . . . began to relate to artists as if they were the central players in any collaboration." Likewise, by making community groups and members a central part of collaborative efforts, museums will overcome the obstacles of ownership, access, and trust that at times have plagued their efforts to position themselves as relevant to community life. To accomplish this, the museum may have to prioritize the relationship with a community over immediate programming needs.

Boundaries and Expectations

Still, as museums seek to play more central roles in strengthening communities, they will need to set clear boundaries. Engaging the community does not mean becoming all things to all people. Shelly Neal, executive director of the Cambridge Multicultural Art Center, notes, "Because [the center] was a community-based institution, people said, 'Yeah, come on; you can do that here.' And then what [we ended] up with [was] exhausted staff. Not a partnership. Not a real organic relationship where there's a give and take, where you develop and you work together. You just use each other. People need to be really clear about what their needs are and what they can and can't do." Otherwise, she says, there will be conflict.

Setting clear boundaries in community work involves managing expectations. "Expectations that you raise in engaging a community in dialogue are not always expectations that you can continue to meet," says Chan. "When do you make it clear that this is a one-time thing? And what is your responsibility, if any, to the lingering impact and subtext of dialogue." If community engagement is going to involve more than a single instance, consistency is important. A museum needs to fulfill its promises. It also must act internally in a way that is consistent with its own public rhetoric. "When you make a commitment to serving multiple communities, there's an expectation that you are really serious," says Doug Wheeler, director of the Washington Performing Arts Society. "Community agencies look to see if [the society] is keeping its commitment institutionally."

In addition, how each staff member approaches his or her individual work will significantly influence what is deemed to be possible for the museum. Many professionals are concerned that expressly recognizing the civic mission will make workloads unbearable at already understaffed nonprofits. Practicing civic engagement should not necessarily translate into more work, particularly since every museum already has a public dimension. Rather, civic engagement should challenge institutions to restructure their priorities and encourage individuals to think about their jobs in different ways.

Flexibility and Risk-Taking

As the museum connects more deeply with its community, one certainty is that its leaders and stakeholders will need to keep learning. In particular, challenges should be seen as opportunities to create new ways of fulfilling the museum's goals. In other words, museums will have to develop a certain amount of resiliency. As Ben Cohen of Ben and Jerry's Ice Cream says, "To stumble is not to fall but to move forward more quickly."[6]

Reflecting on the Washington Performing Arts Society's history with community programming, Kim Chan says, "We were all experimenting. No one really knew how to make these kinds of partnerships work. [We] were kind of working on gut instinct." According to the society's director, the risk was worth it. Says Wheeler: "It often pays to stick your neck out once in a while."

The Cambridge Multicultural Arts Center approaches its mission to fight racism and bigotry in the same way, says former co-chair Janis Pryor. "I was not about to set us up by saying come to our dialogues and the problem of racism will be solved," she says. "Because this is a problem that has been going on for hundreds of years, and we're not about to solve it in one dialogue. We were very clear that we were going into new territory and that we'd have fits and starts."

The value of organizational learning also comes through in the Everett Dance Theatre's rehearsal process. At rehearsals, Artistic Director Dorothy Jungels pays special attention to mistakes, experiments, and diversions, as well as others' perceptions of what the dance should be. For example, during the rehearsal for *Pandora's Restaurant*, says Jungels, "all this vitality started to happen—this truthfulness, this honesty, this surprise." Many of those new ideas were incorporated into the final production.

Museums that develop a willingness to learn—especially from their mistakes—are more likely to approach each community partnership in a unique way allowing for more of a give-and-take in their community relationships.

Recommendations

Museums engaging in self-reflection and connecting with community members and organizations soon will find that patience is a required virtue; over time, they will develop rich internal and community relationships grounded in trust. But museums also can take some immediate steps to support their efforts. Institutionalizing community engagement efforts, from the leadership down, seems to increase the sustainability of the initiatives. Museums also should ensure that the success of their community work does not depend on any one personality but on the members of the various departments and the staff's understanding of the projects.

Organizational stakeholders—in museums, this means the board—should undergo a similar process. "If you can't engage the board of a nonprofit in those issues," say Chan, an organization "will continually be unsuccessful or . . . never fully institutionalize dialogue with its community." The Cambridge Multicultural Art Center's early work with its board led directly to the development of community dialogues. "I felt that if we were going to engage in a dialogue on race and arts as an institution, we had to do the same work ourselves," says Pryor.

Institutionalization increases the strength and stability of organizational commitment and helps to ensure the consistency of arts-based civic dialogue programming. "Ultimately, the goal of such partnerships is that they become independent of the individuals involved," says Abel Lopez, associate director of the GALA Hispanic Theater in Washington, D.C.[7] To be successful, efforts to engage in issues that influence or shape community health must reside in the structures of the organization. As museums continue to develop their skills in civic engagement, their leaders should involve a wide range of board and staff in such efforts, to ensure that the skills individuals develop become a part of relevant organizational systems. The more staff are involved, the greater the likelihood that critical skills will be infused into the museum's institutional memory, thus creating the opportunity for meaningful engagement in the future.

Museums have successfully reinvented themselves over the past 25 years, establishing themselves as educators and stewards of our intellectual heritage. Museum professionals have succeeded in adjusting their focus and operations to support a redefined mission. As museums now explore the principles and practices that support dynamic engagement with communities and become civic enterprises, an appreciation of the role of organizational culture can prove invaluable. Organizational culture is a phenomenon that surrounds all that a museum does. Certain aspects of culture are not directly perceptible, but they nonetheless drive and are reflected in the actions taken by an organization. Museums' efforts to become visible and central players in civic life will be aided by a strong, integrated culture that supports vision, purpose, and goals. As Herb Kelleher, CEO of Southwest Airlines, says, "Culture is one of the most precious things a company has, so you must work harder on it than anything else." [8]

References

1. Edgar Schein, *Organizational Culture and Leadership* (San Francisco: Jossey-Bass, 1985).

2. Richard Evans and Laurel Jones, *Beyond Stabilization: Arts Funding and Organizational Development* (San Francisco: The Bay Group International, 1996).

3. Deborah Jowitt, "Work Force," *Village Voice*, Feb. 20, 1996.

4. Marty Pottenger, "Letter from an Artist: Marty Pottenger," Nov. 11, 2001: www.communityarts.net/readingroom/archive/27pottenger.php.

5. Barbara Schaffer Bacon, Cheryl Yuen, and Pam Korza, *Animating Democracy: The Artistic Imagination as a Force in Civic Dialogue* (Washington, D.C.: Americans for the Arts, 1999).

6. National Endowment for the Arts," Innovation and Entrepreneurship" in *Reassessment of Support for National Organizations: Colloquia Summaries*, March 3, 2000: www.arts.endow.gov/explore/Colloquia/capitalization.html.

7. Rose Solari, "Long-Term Commitments and One-Night Stands," *Inside Arts*, July 1998: www.wpas.org/InsideArt.html.

8. "The Culture of Choice: Assessing and Aligning Culture" (Foster City, Calif.: Hagberg Consulting Group, Jan. 27, 2002): http://w3.hcgnet.com/culture_main.html.

Daniel Kertzner is a program coordinator in the Communities Department, Massachusetts Cultural Council, Boston.

HOW COMMUNITY FOUNDATIONS CAN HELP MUSEUMS FULFILL THEIR CIVIC MISSIONS
. . . .

By Mariam C. Noland and Katie M. Goatley

Museums and community foundations share an important similarity—at the core of business for both is the civic mission of building community. Both types of institutions have histories that support this ideal, and both live in a present where it becomes more important every day. Both are nonprofit organizations, working for the public good. Both know that strengthening cultural ties and facilitating cross-cultural understanding is critical to successful community change. What is only now being recognized, however, is that museums and community foundations can partner in innovative ways to leverage the necessary resources for pursuing their civic missions. In metropolitan Detroit, for example, the Community Foundation for Southeastern Michigan (CFSEM) helped the Henry Ford Museum & Greenfield Village and the Arts League of Michigan collaborate on a greater mission to build community and realize some immediate, practical goals in the process.

First some history: The museum has long been part of the Detroit community family. It was founded in 1929 as the Edison Institute (a K-12 school whose mission was to introduce students to American innovation, ingenuity, and resourcefulness) and opened to the public eight years later. Today, the Henry Ford Museum & Greenfield Village has a collection of more than 1 million artifacts, 26 million documents, and 90 historic structures, highlighting both famous American inventors and the ordinary people whose lives were changed by new technologies. With more than 1.5

million visitors from around the world, the museum is one of the most visited cultural sites in North America.

While the museum had good reasons to be proud of its global connections, a few years ago staff began to think about how they could improve their ties to the local community. Metropolitan Detroit has a high percentage of African-American residents; yet in the early 1990s less than 5 percent of the museum's visitors were minorities. The museum had long sought to attract more African Americans—as staff, volunteers, and audience members. But anecdotal evidence suggested that African Americans in the area believed that the museum focused solely on the history and accomplishments of white America and did not relate to people of color. And though the local Dearborn community had evolved from a blue-collar, white, working-class community into one of the most diverse areas in the region, the city was perceived by local African Americans as unwelcoming.

In an effort to become relevant to all citizens in the Detroit area, the museum developed a strategic plan in the late 1990s. The plan called on the museum to "contribute to community improvement in the realms of education, economic development, and quality of life" in metropolitan Detroit. It also called for increasing the ethnic and racial diversity of museum stakeholders. Visitor surveys revealed that to attract more families and minority groups, the museum would have to change how it was perceived in the community—i.e., enhance its existing programs and develop new ones.

The Henry Ford Museum realized it could accomplish its goal to better engage its community only by forming meaningful relationships with community-based organizations. In this case, that meant collaborating with the Detroit-based Arts League of Michigan. Established in 1991, the Arts League serves as an advocate for local African-American cultural arts and, through collaborations and partnerships, helps establish and promote black artists inside and outside the African-American community. By trying to unite diverse groups of people, the Arts League seeks to benefit the greater Detroit community.

With a mutual goal to make both institutions more diverse, the museum and the Arts League developed a plan to more accurately represent African-American history at the museum. Both organizations believed that would increase their value as true community institutions. But where would they find the funds to accomplish this objective?

Part of that answer came in 1999 in the form of a $250,000 multi-year grant from CFSEM. The grant allowed the museum and the Arts League to imbue their institutions with living history. They focused on the story of the Harlem Renaissance—from the perspective of the Detroit community—and its connection to Idlewild, a northern Michigan resort that was a haven for black artists and intellectuals in the 1920s and '30s. The museum and the Arts League developed outdoor theatrical presentations, an annual program during Black History Month that highlights the major figures and achievements of the Harlem Renaissance, and oral-history projects that encourage families to research their own ties to the Idlewild resort. They also took actors portraying figures from the Harlem Renaissance to schools, libraries, and faith-based community institutions.

As a result of these efforts, the museum became a more welcoming place to previously underserved audiences, as evidenced by the significant increase in the number of African Americans involved in the institution. Members of the community who had felt excluded now could see themselves represented in the institution, as could the museum's traditional constituents. The new stakeholders not only were given the opportunity to share their stories but also could see them embraced and given increased value by the greater Detroit community. The collaboration allowed the museum to move toward the center of community life. And the Arts League was able to initiate and strengthen relationships with individuals outside its own core constituency.

That the Henry Ford Museum and the Arts League—two very different organizations (in terms of size, mission, resources, etc.)—could successfully collaborate on a cultural topic sent a significant message to the Detroit community, where racial conflict is a major challenge. Leaders at the museum and the league pledged to continue to look for ways to collaborate with new and different partners and to broaden their horizons in the community.

In other words, everyone—most particularly the citizens of Detroit— benefited either directly or indirectly from the project. That is because, in the end, it did more than aid the Henry Ford Museum and the Arts League, it built "social capital." In *Culture Matters: How Values Shape Human Progress*, Francis Fukuyama defines social capital as a "set of informal values of norms shared among members of a group that permits them to cooperate with one another."[1] This cooperation helps to create a framework for linking people to each other and, as a result, creating positive change in the community. Community foundations build social capital by leveraging human and financial resources from many sectors and targeting them toward activities that bring together dissimilar groups and individuals to effectively build and sustain community. They also recognize that arts and culture organizations can make an enormous contribution to the community—more than they are doing now. That is why many community foundations have identified "arts and culture" as a key area for funding. But unless museums recognize and act upon their civic mission, those funds will continue to be unavailable to them.

Another social-capital success story involving arts and culture centers on the Concert of Colors Festival and Concert Series in Detroit. The grantee for this project was the Arab-American Community Center for Economic and Social Services (ACCESS), located in Dearborn. The largest Arab-American human service agency in the country, ACCESS serves one of metropolitan Detroit's largest minority groups, comprising some 300,000 persons of Arab descent. Cultural programming is an integral part of the organization's community offerings, and includes the Arab International Festival, held each summer in Dearborn, which celebrates Arab heritage and attracts more than 150,000 people.

Cultural organizations in the Detroit region have not been particularly successful in expanding their reach beyond their own natural constituencies. It is true that organizations representing minority communities broaden the scope of their work and expand their cultural programming as the size of their populations increase. But major nonprofits, including arts and cultural organizations, have been slow to seek advice and participation from minority communities. In addition, leadership in racial and ethnic communities has not always felt welcome at "mainstream" arts and cultural events, which would help make those cultural activities more familiar and less intimidating to people of color. Staff at ACCESS realized the solution to the problem was to enhance the city's social capital. In the late 1990s, the organization applied for a grant from CFSEM that would allow it to demonstrate how Detroit could operate as a single community and acknowledge, promote an understanding of, and celebrate the cultural and ethnic differences of local residents.

ACCESS directed its $250,000 grant toward a $1.4-million, multi-year project to promote music of different cultures in Detroit. Since the fall of 1999, an annual series of world music concerts has been held at different venues in the city, as has a free, three-day festival that includes lectures, poetry, film, theater, musical performances, and visual-arts exhibitions in which all the major ethnic groups in metropolitan Detroit are represented. The project is an expansion of the Concert of Colors, a free one-day event held each summer since 1992, and was modeled after the World of Music, Arts, and Dance (WOMAD) festival launched in England in the early 1980s. To complement the local talent, the festival brings world-class performers to the city—European and white American artists as well as the Asian, African, Latino, and Native American artists traditionally included in the Concert of Colors. In addition to the festival, each year area cultural organizations stage several other world music concerts. For example, in February 2000, the Caribbean Carnival attracted nearly 1,500 metro-area Detroiters to the suburban Royal Oak Music Theater. And the local Association of Chinese Americans helped bring the Peking Opera to the city in March 2000.

Because of the CFSEM grant, ACCESS and its partners were able to strengthen their ethnically specific cultural programming and build bridges between ethnic groups and mainstream organizations. The festival became an important part of community life. It also exemplified how organizations can come together and share their assets, resources, and constituencies, allowing everyone to benefit. This was particularly true for the smaller institutions, which due to their increased visibility were afforded new opportunities to form relationships with organizations beyond their traditional sphere of engagement.

Like the hundreds of community foundations across the country, CFSEM strives to improve the quality of life for all who live and work in its geographic region. It does this by encouraging individuals to contribute financial resources to the work of local nonprofit organizations. Over time, these gifts build permanent endowment funds that provide flexible local capital, which both aids the survival of the nonprofit organizations and also serves the public good. Unlike an independent foundation, which often centers its mission around the interests of a single donor, a community foundation is accountable to the entire community, and it must build its mission around the interests of numerous, often thousands, of donors. To balance these interests in an equitable way, the community must be at the table. In some ways, the process used to involve them in the conversation is more important than the potential outcome. Operating in a transparent way and asking for true community participation in the decision-making process is what empowers organizations—including foundations and museums—to say that they are community conscious.

Thus when the foundations do move forward to offer support, they often have the backing of a large and diverse group of community members. When efforts to generate positive change are accompanied by a high level of consensus among community members, they can have a powerful and enormous impact. When their boards, staff, and volunteers embrace the civic mission, museums also can have this kind of transformative effect on the life of their communities.

There are several ways in which community foundations can help museums as they seek to reinvigorate their civic role:

- **Provide incentives to support collaboration.** Some organizations will not move aggressively to build community until they understand that it is in their own self-interest. The first incentive to change can be foundation financial support: grants can help organizations begin to pursue civic engagement, although they cannot and should not be the reason institutions stay in the business of building social capital.

- **Help nonprofits understand the value of building social capital.** Foundations can provide an external point of view that helps nonprofit organizations see the benefits to building social capital. Once organizations understand that building social capital also can help them achieve their mission and goals, they become much more interested.

- **Convene likely and unlikely partners.** Perhaps the single best role for community foundations is that of convener. Though a foundation can offer seemingly basic motivators for groups to expand the community, these issues require an immense amount of discussion, understanding, and consensus-building before they can occur. But as the aforementioned metropolitan Detroit cases demonstrate, those things will happen when the appropriate venue and structure are offered.

- **Mechanism to build endowment.** Community foundations can help to build the permanent endowments of local nonprofits. And though the endowment itself is important, perhaps more important is the act of getting donors to contribute to the long-term survival of an institution. Assistance to building endowment can be offered in a number of ways. In Detroit, the Hudson-Webber Foundation financially backed CFSEM's efforts to support the planned-giving and endowment-building activities of 19 local, leading cultural organizations. Those organizations received special, targeted training on using planned gifts to build endowments for the organizations. When such gifts are contributed to an endowment, a permanent fund that provides annual income, they help the institution for decades to come.

In return for these types of support, community foundations ask cultural institutions and other nonprofits to embrace the concept of building social capital. Institutions that do this have the unique ability to encourage people to think about issues in a new way, foster dialogue between individuals and institutions that do not traditionally talk to each other, and develop exhibits and ideas that lie outside traditional comfort zones. This, in turn, will help them become important players in changing the face of the community.

Like the civic museum, community foundations strive to develop dynamic relationships with their stakeholders. Though each relationship will take its own shape and form, there are a few characteristics that apply to all. Based on our experience at CFSEM, this is what we have learned:

- **Listen, respond to, and engage communities.** The benefits of engaging in an ongoing dialogue with the community is essential for cultural organizations not only as a survival mechanism (i.e., increased local interest and attendance) but also as a way to broaden their influence over greater societal issues.

- **Create true partnerships with other community members and institutions.** Working with new collaborators—whether they are cultural organizations, individual artists, or government entities—can lead to creative projects. Collaboration also can leverage additional dollars. That said, it should also be noted that partnerships should not be forced. Rather, they should come about when they make sense and when organizations are totally committed to moving forward together. When partnerships work correctly, they can have a much more powerful impact on the community than can one organization working alone.

- **Test innovative solutions to community problems.** It is possible for museums to change the way they work and, at the same time, stay true to their mission. Openness to new ideas is a key ingredient to both forming partnerships and community engagement. Some organizations fear the impact of incorporating differing views. But CFSEM's experience is that organizations that respond to ideas from their communities end up even closer to their missions than when they started—and they have fun and learn a great deal in the meantime!

Public trusts, such as museums and community foundations, have a responsibility to use whatever power and influence they have to bring people together to make their communities a better place to live. Thus, building social capital should be part of what all nonprofit organizations do. While it clearly is in museums' self-interest, it also is the right thing to do.

R e f e r e n c e s

1. Francis Fukuyama, "Social Capital," in *Culture Matters: How Values Shape Human Progress*, ed. Lawrence E. Harrison and Samuel P. Huntington (New York: Basic Books, 2000).

Mariam C. Noland is president, and Katie M. Goatley, is program officer, Community Foundation for Southeastern Michigan, Detroit.

Points of View: Reimagining Museums' Civic Potential

INTRODUCTION
. . . .

Since the Sept. 11 tragedy, museums and museum professionals across the country have become more committed than ever to strengthening their relationships with their communities. As Ellen Hirzy articulates in her essay "Mastering Civic Engagement," they understand that a museum can play a civic role beyond that of cultural symbol, caretaker of collections, educator, and economic engine. Museums can create a strong, positive sense of place, unite people in an effort to strengthen civic and community life, and help members of the community develop leadership skills through their involvement with the institution. They can be places for community forums, providing information and opportunities for dialogue and helping people make decisions about common concerns. Museums can accomplish all of this by learning and mastering civic engagement.

In 2000 and 2001, AAM convened six Museums & Community (M&C) dialogues to stimulate conversations between museum leaders and their counterparts in community organizations. These dialogues confirmed that every museum shapes its own civic role, that communities would like that role to expand, and that museums lie somewhere along a continuum of museum and community engagement. Some museums are systemically engaged with their communities, while at others, the level of engagement depends on the commitment and participation at the individual or departmental level. But wherever an institution is on the continuum of civic engagement, it can enhance its community consciousness by listening deeply and openly to others actively engaged in the same process.

Civic engagement is not easy or instantaneous. It is a highly complex process that by necessity incorporates multiple viewpoints and a willingness to compromise. It requires the ability to grapple with conflicting ideas about how to proceed, and a willingness to accept the ambiguous nature of the process. Museum professionals who respond to their communities by initiating change within their institutions appear to reap significant benefits for the museum, the staff, and the board. Civically engaged museums serve the public better and see increases in their attendance and credibility, employee productivity and morale, and community support.

"Points of View" comprises 10 personal reflections by M&C dialogue participants from around the country, who discuss their experiences with learning and mastering civic engagement and provide perspectives on reimagining museums' civic potential. These brief essays demonstrate that one size does not fit all, that every individual and institution approaches civic engagement differently; and offer insights for other organizations seeking to connect with their communities. As Kathleen Stiso Mullins writes in "Looking Outward," museums need to be "more inclusive, more responsive, more relevant, and more connected. . . ." This may require a shift in thinking—each museum developing its own evolving model for civic engagement, and continuing to learn, experiment, and transform.

EXTENDING A WELCOME
. . . .

By Charles K. Steiner

Architecture conveys critical messages about a museum's character and function. The Wichita Art Museum is expanding its 1977 building, designed by Edward Larrabee Barnes. At the same time, it is making the transition from a municipal museum to a private museum. Director Charles K. Steiner reflects on the physical and fiscal transformations, both of which affect the museum's public face and civic purpose.

For 25 years the Wichita Art Museum didn't have a welcoming entrance. To get into the 1977 Barnes building, visitors had to drive up a hill and walk by a fountain. No one anticipated the Kansas wind blowing the water from the fountain all over the clothes of museum visitors. To make matters worse, the fountain leaked into the room below. The arrival routine was complicated: Drivers would drop their passengers at the door, go back down the hill to park, and then climb some very steep stairs over a berm to get into the building. It wasn't, in fact, very accessible or very welcoming, and because the original entrance didn't work, the museum started using the ground-floor door next to the loading dock in full view of a dumpster.

Our current expansion will change all that. Even while our building is closed during construction, we've begun to present a different face to the community. We invited the Northeast Magnet School here in Wichita to create an artwork on our construction fence. The students ended up doing 6-by-8-foot plywood Louise Nevelson-like relief sculptures that were too heavy for the fence, so we placed them among the trees around the building. Similarly, the parents, teachers, and students of one of the private schools in town, Wichita Collegiate School, made art projects out of those plastic lawn geese, and we must have shown about 75 of them at our annual holiday event. I'm hoping to integrate other community-inspired outdoor installations that send the message—before people even go into the building—that we're interested in community involvement and that the museum is a lively place.

The new entrance, which will have two works by Dale Chihuly, will open into a 6,500-square-foot great hall where community groups will be able to hold meetings. We're also going to have two meeting rooms that community groups can rent. We're moving our interactive gallery up from the basement to the first floor into an expanded space, and we're trying to make it less static. We're calling it the Living Room, as a way of attracting people of all ages—not just children, not just adults, not just adults with children. We'll also expand our gallery space by 40 percent. We'll devote more space to our regional collection, artists who maybe are not nationally known but for whom there is a certain fondness and loyalty here in the community.

Privatization presents an interesting paradox. On the one hand the city, and my own values, would dictate that we should be trying to interest all facets of the community in the museum and perhaps extend the museum out into the community. But on the other hand, those areas of the community that we all want to serve the most are really in the least position to pay for services. There's a strong mandate to fund the museum with private dollars, but those dollars are not going to come from the political constituency that the city cares most about. It's absolutely critical to keep the city government financially involved with the museum. Privatization is a good idea in principle, but if it goes too far we close out the very resources that will fund and ensure that there's full community involvement.

I feel that I'm coming full circle on this idea of museums and community. I started my museum career as a Rockefeller Foundation Fellow at the Metropolitan Museum of Art right after the exhibition "Harlem on My Mind" in the late 1970s. The late Howard Klein conceived the fellowship program as a way of infusing art museums with staff from spheres of the community where museums had not been recruiting staff. His theory was that the fellows would serve as a personnel pool from which traditionally elitist art museums would draw in subsequent years. So I feel that the notion of an expanded civic or community role was born at the beginning of my career, and that it then subsided, and now is coming back in a different form.

COMMUNITY ROOTS
. . . .

By Ron Chew

Community-based museums like the Wing Luke Asian Museum in Seattle have useful lessons to impart about civic engagement. Director Ron Chew advocates an infusion of nontraditional strengths and skills, because staff who can shape a vibrant civic role for a museum may not necessarily come from the usual backgrounds.

The whole process of creating a different kind of museum—a community-rooted museum—begins with the hiring of people with different kinds of skills. At the Wing Luke Asian Museum, we value community involvement, organizing skills, and experience in settings where collective decision making is used. We look for those qualities over some of the specific talents that traditional museums look for, such as academic training or subject-matter knowledge. In the long run, you're trying to build lasting community linkages. Larger museums are seeking to emulate community-based museums by extending tentacles into many places, so that the strength of the organization is not built on a few small connections, but fed by a whole network of roots.

When you come into a museum without specific training or experience in the profession—as many of us social activists did—you're trying to figure it out for yourself, and then trying to guide your staff as well. It's a tricky balance. You're intensely aware of your symbolic role as a leader, but you're also a student and learner. You learn, for example, how other museums develop their exhibitions, but you don't want to be shackled by their traditional approaches, which often mute or ignore the stories, personal perspectives, and topical concerns of people in the community. People, not artifacts, are the vital center of a dynamic community-based museum.

At our museum, we've consciously tried to nurture the professional development of the staff. We want to help foster a new generation of museum leaders. This notion of empowering others to carry on the work of the museum comes from our experience as organizers trying to push for grassroots social change, bringing both students and elders together to the table. My work is not necessarily about leaving my own imprint, but about bringing more people into the process and giving them an opportunity for hands-on experience. It is the vision and energy of those who follow me that will breathe new purpose and creativity into our museum.

I've argued strongly that where you make the biggest difference is on the staff level. You can change the board, but ultimately the people who drive the institution, who move it inch by inch forward, are the staff. Unless you have diversity there—unless you have staff with a strong commitment to community, with the skill and stamina to activate relationships—your board is not going to be able to overcome that deficit. We value the relationships that people bring to the institution. If they participate in their church, in service organizations or in volunteer projects, or things like that, they're strengthening the community at the same time that they're building bridges back into the museum.

Some museums set up advisory boards to fill in the gap, but I see these as token groups that rubber-stamp internal decisions made within the museum's administrative structure. It's important to keep in mind that there has to be real transfer of power and meaningful input from outside the museum, because that's what builds a healthy, vibrant institution. Having an advisory board doesn't mean anything just by itself. People are becoming smarter about the need for fair, equitable museum-community relationships—not partnerships of convenience simply set up so that the museum will be the sole beneficiary.

A VISIBLE COMMUNITY CENTER

. . . .

By Rosann Guggino Garcia

The Ybor City Museum Society in Tampa, Fla., is a citizen support organization for a small museum complex, located in a National Historic District that was once the largest cigar production center in the world. With just two full-time staff and a 15-member board, the museum society seeks a stronger civic presence as Ybor City undergoes intensive redevelopment. Rosann Guggino Garcia, board member and immediate past president, describes the society's civic aspirations and relates a preservation success story.

Founded in 1886 by businessman Don Vicente Martinez-Ybor, Ybor City was planned as a cigar-manufacturing town. Don Vicente's Land and Improvement Company, which included his colleagues, actively sought out other factory owners, built shotgun single-family homes for workers, and recruited all the support services and businesses needed by the newly formed town.

Decades later, Ybor City had become almost a ghost town; the vibrant shopping, entertainment, and residential community had moved to the suburbs after the decline of the cigar industry. In the early 1990s, the city's redevelopment started with a campaign to lure businesses back, but it soon got out of hand. Liquor licenses were handed out freely and crowds started frequenting the bars. Rents were raised, driving artists and small shop owners away; and big business stepped in to build an entertainment district.

Often compared to New Orleans's Bourbon Street and French Quarter, the Ybor night scene attracts a crowd that contributes nothing to the preservation of the city's historic district.

In addition, the redevelopment of Ybor City—a combined public-private investment of about $200 million—didn't include the promotion of Ybor's history in a significant way. For the first time anywhere in the United States, a National Historic Landmark District was in danger of losing its integrity and many historic homes and neighborhoods. That's where the Ybor City Museum Society stepped in.

The museum's mission is to actively promote the rich ethnic diversity of the city's "Latin" community, to preserve and interpret the contributions and the stories of the Spanish, the Italian, the Jewish, and the Cuban communities and the heritage of Ybor City, and to protect the community's history through a highly visible presence in the Tampa/Ybor City region. Our civic role is to make sure that that heritage survives the redevelopment of the community. We're not even close to being on the lips of the community, so we have a very big job to do. Our responsibility is to link what we've learned from the past to how we deal with the present. We could be a community center, a place that's alive and thriving.

To protect Ybor's heritage, we began a five-year growth plan in 1998, with the knowledge that we needed to become a driving force in the city. We're establishing that focus by presenting programming and exhibits involving community members, who not only have stories to tell but have current needs and interests the museum could meet. We're calling on people to suggest what they'd like to see in our museum, what topics they want to explore, and what aspects of their personal history they want represented. We have touched on all of the cultures that have made up the Ybor community since its founding in 1886. Right now we're focusing on the matriarchs of the community.

When you bring people in and ask them what they want out of the museum and involve them in the decision making, you empower the community. They feel that they have a say in what's going on in this history museum. There are some distasteful subjects in the history of Ybor City, and it's our responsibility as a museum to report those things: the political upheavals, the anti-Spanish movement, the labor conditions in the cigar factories. Illegal gambling, prostitution, and gang-style murders tarnished the reputations of innocent Tampa Latins, as well as the guilty. These topics raise eyebrows, and you don't make friends all the time. But your purpose is to educate.

When final plans were presented for the expansion of Interstate 4 through Ybor City, the museum stepped forward with a project—a very special partnership [designed] to ameliorate the impact of the expansion. The Federal Highway Administration, Florida Department of Transportation, City of Tampa, and Hillsborough County government agreed to save as many of the historic homes as possible, relocate them onto vacant lots on the north side of the interstate, and renovate them for residential use—a project that all these government agencies endorsed as Las Casitas Project.

As a result, the Ybor Museum Society will receive five historic and architecturally important homes, which will be placed on land across the street and next to the museum. The city and county are providing the site, and the Department of Transportation is renovating the homes. The project re-creates a turn-of-the-century streetscape in the middle of the business district, and it supports the society's mission to preserve and protect the heritage of Ybor City. The houses will be leased to small businesses, provide an income stream, and generate activity and more foot traffic into the museum's neighborhood. The Ybor City Museum State Park and Las Casitas complex will create major visibility in the community. We will become a part of the city's economic development. And we'll show that economic development can work hand in hand with preserving the community's history.

CIVIC ENGAGEMENT STARTS WITH THE BOARD

. . . .

By Ron L. Kagan

A museum's board shapes, reflects, and advocates the institution's values. Ron L. Kagan, director of the Detroit Zoological Institute and Society, suggests that a civic-minded museum should have a board that represents "the hearts and minds of the entire community." Museums typically listen intently to their supporters, users, and members, but that approach needs to change.

Our challenge really starts not with who has voice, but with who has votes. Those two things aren't necessarily the same, and they don't have to be. We need to look not just for more diverse voices but for more diverse voting. It's not just about race, religion, gender, and age. It's about having the entire community's hearts and minds represented in the most critical decision-making forum—the board of a museum.

This is not to suggest that political and affluent civic leaders aren't wonderful. But there naturally tends to be greater allegiance to users than to nonusers, and the only way you get people to be users is if they feel that the museum is relevant and a part of their community experience. Museums can be self-reinforcing, closed environments.

When we started the discussions about who to invite to the Detroit dialogue, we were all alarmingly unsure of who actually represents the community and what defines community. This illustrates that we have an unclear view about whom we should be talking with, and it probably reflects the absence of full understanding about who might be interested, able, and willing to contribute. In my view, we have to question whether we're even capable of having this dialogue with our communities unless our internal decision-making positions become much more diverse.

The soul searching within the profession and within museums is very important. About 10 years ago when government funding started to dry up, many institutions started talking about their relevance to the community because we couldn't take anything for granted. There's been an encouraging evolution, and there is less elitism as a result. But my guess is that we're not likely to see any kind of quantum leap in this area unless we have some really outstanding leadership and all of us broaden our understanding about board participation and representation. It's extremely difficult for the CEO or the senior staff of an institution to talk with boards on this issue—to say, basically, you need to give up some of your power to people who don't give money or aren't traditional power brokers or politicians.

I think about how passionate people are about sports, how important sports are in our daily lives. Clearly that loyalty is something powerful, and we ought to be aiming our cultural sector toward that kind of bond. The only thing that even comes close is the commitment that many people make to their religions and places of worship.

Zoos and aquariums are fortunate because, for the most part, our attendance figures are significant, and we tend to be stronger magnets than other cultural institutions because of the way people seem to connect with animals. For example, we know that the accredited zoos in the United States actually have a larger annual audience than professional sports.

But all museums tend to shape very unique memories and experiences, and that's a very powerful capacity in and of itself. Yet we haven't gotten to the point where we inspire the same kind of loyalty as the public gives to sports teams. Museums tend to listen to their users but, of course, that's usually a small sector of the entire community. If we're going to engage the public and take on a more prominent civic role, we need to listen not just to members, visitors, and patrons, but to all people who could benefit from what we do and might very well develop that loyalty to museums if we just invited them in. And along with a voice, we need to then provide some votes, too.

LOOKING FOR REINVENTION

. . . .

By Don Checots

Like museums, public television is involved in a dialogue about its potential for civic engagement and expanded service. Don Checots, president and general manager of KPTS-TV in Wichita, Kans., talks about the parallels—and the potential for collaboration—between the two fields.

In this discussion of museums and civic engagement, you could substitute "public television" for "museum" just about anywhere. We are struggling with the same kinds of problems. We've got this tremendous potential because of our delivery system, which literally reaches into everybody's home. But our public television system has relied on a core of programming, and it's beginning to get stale.

In Wichita, KPTS has been pretty invisible for the last decade, relying on its past programming successes, mostly national productions. The station never became the community resource it could be, but we're changing that through a variety of ways that will make KPTS an important local educational and cultural asset. For example, our community wants to see people of all ethnic backgrounds on television—as heroes, as people with important stories to tell, as positive role models. To meet that need, in September 1999, we launched *zygo*, the only locally produced program that focuses on the concerns and interests of people of color.

I feel that museums, too, have relied a lot on what they have done in the past. People who live here in Wichita have said to me, "I've been to the museum." It's the same with public television. People tend to quit sampling us after a while, and then they forget about us. Those who continue to investigate us find new things all the time.

So, like museums, public television is looking for reinvention. We're wondering what we're going to be like a few years from now—especially as digital technology gives us a larger, more flexible delivery system—and how we can be more effective at civic engagement and building social capital. The truth is we have never met our potential, and we need to take a hard look at these issues in ways that may not be comfortable.

Partnering provides a solution. I think there are ways that museums and public television can blend our enterprises to enhance the effectiveness of both. For example, a museum could use television programming to supplement learning and enrich viewing experiences. KPTS's digital technology will allow for the creation of "enhanced" television programs. That means that we could air a program showing artwork and, much like Web-based material, provide additional information about individual pieces, artists, and, techniques, etc., through our digital signal. Digital technology also will allow us to move into wireless, broadband educational opportunities that might include taking learning activities and viewing experiences to rural areas, thereby introducing collections and exhibits to even greater numbers of people. The possibilities are endless.

Museums and public television are on the same track, with the same potential to help people in our communities focus on what's really significant in our lives. I urge museums to learn more about public T.V.'s educational strategies. That process could lead to collaborations and partnerships that better serve all our constituents.

FORGING A TRUE PARTNERSHIP

. . . .

By Dale Thompson

Art ConText, a four-year collaboration between the Providence, R.I., Public Library and the RISD Museum, involves an artist-in-residence program in neighborhood library branches. Library Director Dale Thompson says the relationship with the museum and the artists has convinced her that museums and libraries can combine their strengths in ongoing efforts to benefit their communities.

For the public library, civic engagement is just part of our nature—the relationships that we have with the community and the neighborhoods. The essence of public library service is that each individual's needs are different, and each individual's needs are met. People come in, we know their names. We strive to understand community needs and try to gear our programs and services closely to those needs. That was what the RISD Museum saw when we sat down to talk about our collaboration. We went into it feeling that we were both going to benefit, although in different ways. RISD clearly "got it," and they have been such incredible, outstanding partners.

By linking the library and the museum, Art ConText strengthens the capacity of both institutions. The artists add a wonderful new dimension to the library's focus on literacy, and the museum introduces art—and practicing artists—to people who might not have encountered this kind of experience before. Artists-in-residence spend part of their residencies in a library branch interacting with the public directly in various kinds of programs. I remember when Rebecca Belmore created a photomural called *on this ground* in an empty lot behind the Smith Hill branch. Volunteers from the neighborhood, which is known as the "Little United Nations," helped Rebecca and RISD students transform the lot into a garden. When the mural was finished, we celebrated with an event that the museum's David Henry called "Art Meets Weiner Roast": We roasted hot dogs, planted a "community tree," and listened to music and a Native American storyteller.

Our librarians have had the opportunity to work with the RISD staff very closely. Otherwise, we couldn't have understood the museum the way we do now. Our staff has the opportunity to meet and work with artists on a human level—to really make a connection with art, to see how art can affect the community, to find out that artists are bright, and they're warm, and they're human, and they're women, and they grew up in India, and so on. We've made a connection with a dimension of our lives that we would not have had without our relationship with the museum.

The museum's grant from the Pew Charitable Trusts was for four years, and the extended time period has had a tremendous impact. We've been able to try a lot of different things because we've had long-term funding. This is something new for all of us—the artists, the museum staff, and the library staff. We're constantly learning: What is it that we're looking for? How do we need to work with the artists? What kind of a relationship with the community is most successful?

I sense that some museums tend to have one or two projects but not ongoing relationships. With RISD, we want to do things differently, so we're already thinking about the next step after Art ConText. The library is renovating all of its branches, and in two neighborhoods we're building new branches. One of the things I'd like to do is provide a museum space where RISD and other museums can run programs in the branches. We're just beginning to talk about the possibilities, but we're both interested. We're going to work something out and, based on our experience with Art ConText, I'm sure it's going to be spectacular and wonderful.

BUILDING BRIDGES

· · · · · · · · · ·

By Daniel E. Stetson

Maintaining an active community presence is a high priority for the Polk Museum of Art in Lakeland, Fla. Executive Director Daniel E. Stetson describes the consistent cultivation of attitudes, efforts, and relationships that supports civic engagement.

Polk County, Fla., is a rural county about the size of Connecticut. Our graduation and literacy rates are below the national average, and these are issues of real concern. One answer is to have the arts be an accessible change agent. The museum is open seven days a week for free now. We just added the seventh day because we didn't like seeing people walk away on Mondays. The cost ends up being a small loss for a great gain. Access and comfort of access aren't about niche marketing. If you approach it that way, engagement becomes episodic rather than systemic. The question is, How do you get the general population interested in the museum's general program?

I like the idea of the museum becoming the community's front porch. We use the phrase, "More than an art museum." That's a simple statement with profound meaning. We can be a carnival, a nightclub, a theater—that's the character of an active, fully engaged contemporary museum. As a "vision partner" in a vision planning initiative for the city of Lakeland, the museum has taken on the project of a diversity dialogue series. We recently hosted the first dialogue in the museum with representatives from the local

African-American community. By putting ourselves in the role of convener, we're starting to bring together people and groups in Lakeland who had never met and talked about a vision for their city in the context of an arts institution.

We have 25 staff members, and they have quite a range of skills and talents. Many of the people that we've been fortunate to hire, frankly, were not necessarily involved in art or in this museum. How do you encourage your staff to become engaged in the community in their work? That's something I don't think we have solved entirely. The Lakeland vision plan was reviewed by staff and adopted by the board, and elements of it are specifically tied to our long-range plan. So the staff knows that the museum's goals relate to and support the community's goals. The staff who are involved in the diversity dialogues are empowered to represent the museum as ambassadors. I'm going to assign some relationship building so that we can find out what churches the community participants go to, what fraternal organizations they belong to, and so forth. We're going to work on traveling and talking—not just connecting by phone or by e-mail.

Civic engagement is about bridge building, and then walking over the bridge. And if the bridge gets torn down, you build a new one in the same place but move it over a little bit, and keep doing it again and again. You have to know that to create common ground you must be willing to trust. You get past purely programmatic approaches to engagement through risk taking. And risk taking is generous, because it only feeds you back.

A PUBLIC SERVICE RESPONSIBILITY

. . . .

By Irene Hirano

Applying the lessons of history is embedded in the mission of the Japanese American National Museum. In describing the immediacy of this mission after Sept. 11, Director Irene Hirano suggests that public service is not just an option for museums, but an obligation.

Regardless of what kind of museum it is, part of the role of a nonprofit organization is to be a good community partner. We talk a lot about corporate responsibility, but it seems to me that museums have the same responsibility as organizations to contribute to their communities. That's a pretty powerful statement for the museum field to make: that we have a responsibility as community partners and that each museum must find the best ways to do that. But it is part of the public service that we should expect of ourselves.

Because Japanese Americans had experienced discrimination following the outbreak of World War II—which ultimately led to the incarceration of 120,000 people—the ethnic tensions related to Arab Americans and Muslims after Sept. 11 resonated with us and were of great concern. We saw a responsibility to provide a forum that would enable people to talk about these issues and enable us to share our historical knowledge, mostly through personal stories.

We looked at our public programs schedule and considered what we'd like to do. At the same time, we saw this as part of the ongoing work of our museum. An important role that we can play is to be a place for that kind of dialogue. We felt that we had a responsibility to speak out about lessons that are part of our history and how they can be applied today. We approached public radio station KPCC-FM and suggested that we co-host a town hall meeting that could look at ethnic tension, U.S. security, and civil liberties and how we as a community respond. We knew that the museum could play a role in the healing process.

The two-hour town hall meeting was broadcast live from the museum on "Talk of the City" on the evening of Oct. 11. It was aired again later due to popular demand from the radio station's listeners. The program, which dealt with contemporary issues, included an Arab American leader, a Japanese American who talked about what his family went through right after the start of WWII, and someone from the FBI who talked about racial profiling. We tried to find immediate partners and tapped into their listenership while reaching out to our supporters. The program enabled people to talk about some of what they were feeling, since a town hall is a great opportunity for that kind of dialogue to take place.

Now we're in the process of planning a five-part series using a similar format. It is going to explore the role of museums in exploring the lessons of history and connecting them to current issues. We're going to hold one program around the anniversary of the 1992 civil unrest in Los Angeles, for example, and we'll close the series on Sept. 11, 2002. It's an opportunity for us to continue bringing together various cultural institutions and museums and to provide a way of engaging the community. That's the thing museums need to think about: What are all the ways that we can stimulate community dialogue? We had an overwhelming response to our town hall meeting, and many of the people who responded might not have participated in our ongoing programming. So for us it was a good step.

Our museum continually asks how we can be of greater service to the community in the broadest sense: the Japanese American community, downtown Los Angeles, the greater L.A. region, and—because we are a national museum—the nation as a whole. What we've found is that people are really looking for safe places, forums that don't advocate a position but really enable dialogue to happen.

EARLY EXPERIENCES

. . . .

By Njia Kai

Community organization leaders are enthusiastic about the possibilities for involvement with museums. Njia Kai, an independent filmmaker and community activist, is the founder and director of CAMP (Cultural Arts Mentorship Program) Detroit, an after-school and full-day summer youth program. After the Detroit community dialogue, she began to see that the possibilities are multidimensional.

CAMP Detroit was established in 1998 to provide young people with access to the many gifted artists, musicians, and entrepreneurs who live and work in our area. Within a year, we had become a sought after, even necessary, community service, providing more than just arts and crafts and recreation. An increasing number of families and children now depend on us to provide a safe and creative space for children during leisure hours.

We have extended our program hours and resources to respond to half-days, whole days, and week-long school breaks. We stretch the budget to provide one-way transportation to assist our working parents. We write proposals and nurture collaborations to maintain our program quality while holding fees paid by parents to 25 to 50 percent of the actual costs.

Over the years, there has only been one young person "lost" from CAMP Detroit. Because of his behavior, we were forced to bar a 12-year-old from our program—a painful decision. After a few months, he stopped showing up around the neighborhood. But when he reappeared two years later, CAMP staff and participants greeted him with lots of hugs. He drew me aside, apologized for his past behavior, and asked if he could join us again. At that moment, I knew that all our efforts to sustain our program had been abundantly rewarded. The young man now takes the bus from school to our program, and then to his foster home, three to five days a week.

Similarly, I think museums can give young people an experience that's not just about visiting, that's not about keeping your hands to yourself or being quiet, but that actually lets them develop a meaningful relationship. The New Detroit Science Center has had a positive impact, because it's very much about involving visitors in the process of learning. It is causing the other museums to look at ways of connecting with their visitors in an interactive way that builds a relationship and causes them to take more of an interest. I'm looking forward to setting up a different kind of experience where young people are somehow engaged in a museum. Young people make excellent volunteers; they love to work, and they need structured activity. They are impressed when adults take the time to talk with them. You can win a lot of loyalty from young people.

For example, CAMP program participants become student members of the Charles H. Wright Museum of African American History, which is located in walking distance of our main site. We often visit the museum for guided tours, arts and educational programming, and special performances. And our young people have provided services for the museum as performers and program support.

But think about how much more could be realized from a CAMP Detroit-museum partnership. Each organization would bring a different set of assets to the table. CAMP Detroit has a constituency of community youth and their families. We have staff, facilities, and programming to support collaborations. We have a cultural arts-centered program that helps young people engage with the resources of our local museums. Museums provide 3-D arts and culture lessons and face-to-face dialogues with artists and scholars. Their exhibitions, media, artifacts, and informed staff tell the story of our shared histories, traditions, and cultures. And their unique settings add depth and clarity to workshops and events. Working together, we can generate positive and memorable experiences that will encourage young people to remain involved.

Museums need to know that they are *community* institutions. You may be accessed by the world, and you may hold treasures that are valuable to international interests, but the underpinning of your success is a strong contact with your community—the community that works in your institution and that keeps you going when other visitors trickle in and out. Somehow, in Detroit, we haven't held on to our feeling of community. We have allowed ourselves to agree that we're just a bunch of isolated people who are afraid of each other, and that's ridiculous.

Children are future visitors, artists, historians, and donors. We need to cultivate their appreciation for the things that will benefit our society. If we really believe that museums are important, and should be lasting, then we have to bring young people in—the earlier the better—and give them some responsibility.

LOOKING OUTWARD

. . . .

By Kathleen Stiso Mullins

Kathleen Stiso Mullins considers Mastering Civic Engagement *a stimulus for "the thought-provoking process of how a museum can become both internally and externally more relevant." In Portsmouth, the rapidly changing coastal New Hampshire city where Strawbery Banke is located, the president and CEO sees ample possibilities for a museum to shape a central civic role.*

Public perception is an important issue for museums. We are perceived as keepers of great collections, as educators, and as tourist attractions, but people often overlook our civic roles as communicators, facilitators, and neutral territories for discussion of critical issues. Museums must work simultaneously on two fronts—internal and external—to change this perception. Our internal culture should ensure that we are always looking outward, which means supporting and encouraging staff to be involved in building community, not just through involvement with other cultural and historical organizations, but also through partnerships with civic, educational, and social service groups. At the same time, we need to encourage our communities to see and use museums differently. The best way to begin is to talk with and listen to our communities, listen to what people want, and find ways to involve them as more than passive visitors or program participants. This means becoming more inclusive, more responsive, more relevant, and ultimately more connected to our communities.

Strawbery Banke was created in 1958 as a result of the post-WWII Federal Urban Renewal Program. Several acres in Portsmouth had been targeted for demolition, but efforts were halted in the oldest section of the city, with 10 acres set aside as a nonprofit. Those 10 acres were ultimately incorporated as Strawbery Banke (the name for the area until the 1650s). Restoration of this area of derelict housing and scrap yards was a locally focused project, with citizens raising the money for restoration of the 43 historic structures and creation of period gardens and lanes. The feelings of ownership were strong and often emotional as they worked to save Strawbery Banke, the surrounding neighborhood, and Portsmouth itself. They were tremendously successful. Today, Strawbery Banke is an AAM-accredited museum, surrounding houses sell for an average of $500,000, and the town is rich with historic charm!

But success often comes with its own set of challenges. For centuries, Portsmouth was a military and port community—the naval shipyard was established here in 1800, Pease Air Force Base was a major employer, and as early as the 17th century the port was welcoming ships from around the world. Today, the shipyard is still active, the air force base has become a technology park, and the port continues to be vital. In addition, the military and blue-collar community—with its many brothels, bars, and boarded up storefronts—has been replaced with expensive housing and upscale retail and restaurants. The technology industry has brought thousands of people to the seacoast region; others are choosing this area for their retirement home; Portsmouth has become a bedroom community for Boston; and thousands of tourists make this historic town on the water a destination year-round.

Unfortunately, neither our newest residents nor the tourists have a memory of what the area was like as recently as 30 years ago. Today they see beautiful parks, a flourishing museum, restored historic structures and a bustling tourist town. But those who grew up here see a community changed in ways they don't always see as positive, making it difficult for them to understand and accept what has emerged from their early efforts to save the historic buildings.

Strawbery Banke was one of the first areas of the community to be restored, with great care given to ensuring the restorations and interpretation were accurate. A truly wonderful institution, the museum allowed the community to remember "the way things used to be." But much of the Strawbery Banke experience depends on having some memory of Portsmouth and the seacoast at the time the museum was created, something new residents and tourists don't possess. New residents often comment that it difficult to get involved with Strawbery Banke, that it is difficult to understand the museum and its mission.

Strengthening our relationship with the community is at the top of our agenda. The museum is currently undertaking an interpretive and physical planning process to create an experience that is more relevant to the visitor and to a growing and changing community. To be sure the changes and enhancements are relevant we are talking with and listening to users and prospective users. We're doing this in a number of ways, such as hosting community gatherings to talk about Strawbery Banke's role in the community, inviting K-12 school representatives to help enhance our programs and services for students and teachers, and asking moms, dads, and kids to help us improve our family programs and services. We are striving to include both new residents and long-time residents in the discussions to bridge the often-present gap between the two groups. We're also organizing community forums to support focused discussion of critical community issues.

Over the past few months, as we have reviewed our mission and vision for the Strawbery Banke of the 21st century, we have come to realize that in many ways the museum represents both the history and the future of the American community. Its stories, buildings, and landscapes reflect American life from the late 17th to the mid 20th centuries, and remind us that, no matter what century, the past and the present interact on a daily basis and history influences community issues and decisions. Listening to our community, we are learning how the museum can serve as a bridge between the past and the future—for our local citizens and for our visitors. We hope that people will use the stories and experiences they encounter at Strawbery Banke to reflect on the past and present of their own communities and help ensure that the American community is strong and thriving for future generations.

CONTRIBUTORS

. . . .

ROBERT R. ARCHIBALD, PH.D., is president and CEO of the
Missouri Historical Society, St. Louis, a museum that regularly facilitates
community discussions of significant issues affecting the people of St. Louis.
He chairs the Museums & Community National Task Force and works with
local, regional, and national organizations to implement changes that will
make our communities better places. A member of the AAM Board of
Directors, he has served as chief elected officer of the American Association
for State and Local History. He is the author of, among other books, *A
Place to Remember: Using History to Build Community*.

CHRISTOPHER T. GATES is president of the National Civic League
(NCL), the nation's oldest organization advocating for the issues of
community and democracy. Prior to accepting this position in 1995, Gates
served as NCL's vice president for eight years. He speaks around the world
on the state of America's democracy, the interaction between citizens and
government, and innovations in community problem-solving and also
provides assistance to communities undertaking strategic-planning projects.
Gates is the founding chairman of the Colorado Institute for Leadership
Training and serves on several other boards, including Independent Sector
and the California Center for Civic Renewal; he also is co-chair of the
Saguaro Seminar, a Harvard University project studying "social capital." He
has a masters in public administration from the John F. Kennedy School of
Government at Harvard University and an honors degree in economics
from the University of Colorado at Boulder.

KATIE M. GOATLEY, program officer at the Community Foundation for Southeastern Michigan, joined the staff in June 1999. She has many years of experience in the nonprofit and policy fields, including consultant to the W. K. Kellogg Foundation's Philanthropy and Volunteerism Division; chief lobbyist for the Maryland Food Committee, where she worked on hunger and poverty issues; and research assistant with the Johns Hopkins University Institute for Policy Studies, where she focused on economic development. Goatley also has served on numerous committees, including the board of directors of the Lutheran Volunteer Corps and as a gubernatorial appointee on the Maryland State Advisory Council for Nutrition. She holds a master's degree in policy studies from Johns Hopkins, a master's in legal and ethical studies from the University of Baltimore, and a bachelor's degree in sociology from Western Michigan University.

ELLEN HIRZY is M&C's consulting writer. For 25 years, she has been engaged in issues related to the evolving role and purpose of museums as public institutions. She has written widely about the museum field and has significant experience in documenting and reporting on the outcomes of group processes. For AAM, she has served as writer of *Excellence and Equity: Education and the Public Dimension of Museums*, project director and principal writer of *Museums for a New Century*, and editor of *Museum News*.

MARIA-ROSARIO JACKSON, PH.D., is a senior research associate and director of the Arts, Culture, and Communities Program at the Urban Institute, Washington, D.C. She also currently serves as principal investigator of the institute's *Arts and Culture Indicators in Community Building Project and Investing in Creativity: A Study of the Support Structure for U.S. Artists*. Over the course of her career, her research has been focused on urban policy, urban poverty, community planning, the role of arts and culture in community building processes and the politics of race, ethnicity and gender in urban settings. She also has participated in research efforts on crime prevention, urban parks, housing de-segregation and multi-cultural teacher education. Jackson earned a master's degree in public administration and community development from the University of Southern California and a doctorate in urban planning from the University of California, Los Angeles.

DANIEL KERTZNER is a program coordinator in the Communities Department of the Massachusetts Cultural Council, where he works to develop advocates for the use of arts and culture to build social capital. Drawing upon his years of experience with nonprofits and volunteers, he works with 24 local cultural councils to expand their capacities to serve as cultural leaders in their communities. He has a degree in organizational behavior and management from Brown University, where his research on organizational culture and arts-based civic dialogue received the Arnold Bennett Award for best honors thesis.

MARIAM NOLAND became the first president of the Community Foundation for Southeastern Michigan (CFSEM), Detroit, in 1985. Since its founding in 1984, CFSEM has made more than 13,800 grants totaling over $100 million. Noland has more than 25 years of experience administering community foundations. She joined the staff of the Cleveland Foundation in 1975 where she served as program officer and secretary/treasurer. In 1981, she became vice president of the Saint Paul Foundation, Saint Paul, Minn. She also served as a member of the Community Initiatives Advisory Committee of the John S. and James L. Knight Foundation, as chair of the Council of Michigan Foundations, and as vice chair of the Council on Foundations. Currently, she is a trustee of Henry Ford Health System and Alma College and a commissioner of Detroit 300. Noland obtained an Ed.M. from Harvard University and a B.S. from Case Western Reserve University.

ACKNOWLEDGEMENTS

The American Association of Museums recognizes and thanks the organizations and donors that have supported the Museums & Community Initiative and its dialogues and publications. Generous support for the initiative itself was provided by the Ford Foundation, John S. and James L. Knight Foundation, Nathan Cummings Foundation, and Wallace Reader's Digest Funds.

The six dialogues at the core of the initiative's research phase could not have succeeded without the support of the following organizations: Rhode Island Historical Society; Brown University; Rhode Island School of Design; Museum of Science and Industry, Tampa; University of Southern California; Charles H. Wright Museum of African American History; and the Japanese American National Museum.

AAM also acknowledges the hard work of the dialogue steering committee co-chairs, whose responsibilities ranged from finding local participants to arranging for meeting sites. We give special thanks to the following individuals for their perseverance and good humor: Murney Gerlach, Wit Ostrenko, Alex Sink, Irene Hirano, Hon. Mark Ridley-Thomas, Christy S. Coleman, Steve Hamp, Ron L. Kagan, Susan Kelly, Robert A. Puckett, Charles K. Steiner, Howard Ellington, Thomas Livesay, Ron Chew, and Jane A. Johnson.

From the start, the Museums & Community Initiative was enthusiastically supported and encouraged by the AAM Board of Directors and Edward H. Able, Jr., the association's president and CEO. The board made a strategic decision to fund the project using AAM resources because of their vision and understanding that civic engagement is critical for the future of the museum field. Their leadership and commitment to the project has been indispensable.

A large-scale undertaking, Museums & Community would not have succeeded without the dedication of the initiative's project team. We would like to take this opportunity to thank them for their accomplishments.

Finally, we acknowledge the extraordinary efforts of AAM's Alexandra Marmion Roosa, project manager for Museums & Community, and Jane Lusaka, assistant director, publications, who helped to produce *Mastering Civic Engagement: A Challenge to Museums*.

Kim Igoe
Project Director
Museums & Community

MUSEUMS & COMMUNITY NATIONAL
TASK FORCE AND STEERING COMMITTEES

. . . .

AAM's Museums & Community Initiative was a collaboration between museum leaders and outside experts. Chaired by Robert R. Archibald, president and CEO of the Missouri Historical Society, the National Task Force provided leadership for the Initiative. It had three committees: a Steering Committee appointed by former AAM Board Chair W. Richard West; a National Advisory Committee of community practitioners and experts on issues related to building and sustaining community; and a National Field Committee with diverse representation from the museum field.

National Steering Committee

Robert R. Archibald, chair, Museums & Community Initiative National Task Force, and president, Missouri Historical Society, St. Louis

W. Richard West, director, National Museum of the American Indian, Smithsonian Institution, Washington, D.C., and former board chair, American Association of Museums, Washington, D.C.

Edward H. Able, Jr., president & CEO, American Association of Museums, Washington, D.C.

Steven Newsome, director, Anacostia Museum and Center for African American History & Culture, Smithsonian Institution, Washington, D.C.

Ellsworth Brown, president & CEO, Carnegie Institute, Pittsburgh

Bonnie Pitman, deputy director, Dallas Museum of Art

Kinshasha Holman Conwill, director emeritus, Studio Museum in Harlem, New York

Malcolm Rogers, director, Museum of Fine Arts, Boston

Irene Hirano, director, Japanese American National Museum, Los Angeles

Marsha Semmel, director & CEO, Women of the West Museum, Boulder

Susanna Torruella Leval, director, El Museo del Barrio, New York

Terry Maple, director & CEO, Zoo Atlanta

Cheryl McClenney-Brooker, director of external affairs, Philadelphia Museum of Art

Sherry Hutt, trustee representative, judge of the Maricopa County Superior Court, Phoenix

National Advisory Committee

There are two categories of National Advisory Committee members: Community Practitioners and Special-Expert Advisors.

COMMUNITY PRACTITIONERS

Steven Bingler, president, Concordia, Inc., Troy, N.Y.

Leslie Durgin, mayor of Boulder (1990-97) and director of the Boulder County Civic Forum

Michael Gallis, principal, Michael Gallis & Associates, Charlotte, N.C.

Sergio M. Gonzales, chief of staff, Miami-Dade County Office of the Executive Mayor

Tullia Hamilton, executive director, St. Louis Community Foundation

Maria-Rosario Jackson, senior research associate and director, Arts, Culture, and Communities Program, Urban Institute, Washington, D.C.

Judith Jedlicka, president, Business Committee for the Arts, Long Island City, N.Y.

Susan Kelly, senior manager, community relations, Target Corporation, East Zone, Minneapolis

Father Richard Lawrence, monsignor, St. Vincent de Paul Parish, Baltimore

Robert McNulty, president, Partners for Livable Communities, Washington, D.C.

Jeffery Soule, policy director, American Planning Association, Washington, D.C.

Stefan Toepler, associate research scientist, Johns Hopkins University, Baltimore

Costis Toregas, president, Public Technology, Inc., Washington, D.C.

SPECIAL-EXPERT ADVISORS

Sherry Salway Black, vice-president, First Nations Development Institute, Fredericksburg, Va.

Denise Scott Brown, principal, Venturi, Scott Brown & Associates, Inc., Philadelphia

Martin Chavez, former mayor, Albuquerque, NMex.

Christopher T. Gates, president, National Civic League, Denver

Yudishthir Raj Isar, director, Cultural Policies for Development, UNESCO, Paris

William E. Strickland, Jr., president & CEO, Manchester Craftsmen's Guild, Pittsburgh

Beth Vanderslice, president, Wired Digital, San Francisco

National Museum Field Representatives Committee

Ruth Abram, CEO & president, Lower East Tenement Museum, New York

Ron Chew, director, Wing Luke Asian Museum, Seattle

Rudyard Cooper, executive director, Omaha Children's Museum

Conrad Froehlich, director, Martin & Osa Johnson Safari Museum, Chanute, Kans.

Janet Gallimore, director, Lake County Discovery Museum, Wauconda, Ill.

Murney Gerlach, former executive director, Rhode Island Historical Society, Providence

David Goudy, director, Montshire Museum of Science, Norwich, Vt.

Jacqueline Gray, former external affairs manager, Field Museum, Chicago

Karla Nicholson, statewide services specialist, Kentucky Historical Society, Frankfort

Wit Ostrenko, president, Museum of Science & Industry, Tampa

Alyce Sadongei, American Indian program coordinator, Arizona State Museum, Tucson

Tania Said, community outreach manager, Center for Education and Museum Studies, Smithsonian Institution, Washington, D.C.

Karina R. Durand Velasco, advisor/director of educational services, Museo Nacional del Virreinato, Tepotzotlán, Mexico

Providence, R.I., Community Dialogue, July 20-21, 2000

LOCAL STEERING COMMITTEE

Murney Gurlach (chair), former director, Rhode Island Historical Society

Ann Brengle, CEO, New Bedford Whaling Museum, New Bedford, Mass.

Lou Casagrande, president, Children's Museum, Boston

Christopher Cox, vice president, Mystic Seaport, Mystic, Conn.

Trudy Coxe, CEO, Preservation Society of Newport County, Newport, R.I.

David Ellis, director, Museum of Science, Boston

Anne Emerson, director, Bostonian Society

Edmund Barry Gaither, director and curator, Museum of the National Center for African American Artists, Boston

Phillip Johnston, director, Museum of Art, Rhode Island School of Design

David Kahn, executive director, Connecticut Historical Society, Hartford

Albert Klyberg, executive director, Heritage Harbor Museum

Patricia McLaughlin, assistant to the mayor, Providence, R.I.

Laura Roberts, consultant and member of the Museum Group, Cambridge, Mass.

Malcolm Rogers, Ana & Graham Gund director, Museum of Fine Arts, Boston

Edward Sanderson, director, Rhode Island Preservation & Heritage Commission

William Simmons, executive vice president for academic outreach and affiliated programs, Brown University

Nondas Voll, director, Fund for Community Progress

Kenneth Yellis, museum director and vice president, International Tennis Hall of Fame

Nina Zannieri, director, Paul Revere Memorial Association, Boston

Tampa Community Dialogue, November 16-17, 2000

LOCAL STEERING COMMITTEE

Wit Ostrenko (co-chair), president, Museum of Science & Industry

Alex Sink (co-chair), past president, Bank of America

Dan Bebak, executive director, Mote Marine Aquarium, Sarasota, Fla.

Louis G. Betz, Jr., president, Duck Tours of Tampa Bay, Inc.

Melinda Chavez, former executive director, Ybor City Museum Society, Fla.

Cynthia Gandee, executive director, Henry B. Plant Museum

Terisa Glover, executive director, Explorations V Children's Museum, Lakeland, Fla.

Stephen M. Goldman, director, Florida Holocaust Museum, St. Petersburg

Susan S. Gordon, executive director, Science Center of Pinellas County, St. Petersburg

Mark Greutzmacher, executive director, Tampa Bay History Center

Dick Johnston, president, Florida International Museum, St. Petersburg

Malinda J. Horton, executive director, Florida Association of Museums, Tallahassee

Emily S. Kass, director, Tampa Museum of Art

Nancy Kirk, board member, Terrace Community School

Charlene J. Lawson, former administrative director, Bok Tower Gardens, Lake Wales, Fla.

Jan Luth, vice president of programs, Museum of Science & Industry

Michael Milkovich, director, Museum of Fine Arts, St. Petersburg

Margaret Miller, director, USF Contemporary Art Museum

Kathleen Monahan, community affairs administrator, Tarpon Springs Cultural Center, Fla.

Robert Patterson, director, Great Explorations, St. Petersburg

Craigh Pugh, vice president for advancement, Lowry Park Zoological Garden

Susan Repetto, director, risk management services, Davis Baldwin, Inc.

T. Marshall Rousseau, executive director, Salvador Dali Museum, St. Petersburg

John Ruzic, owner, Best Western

C. Lex Salisbury, president/CEO, Lowry Park Zoological Garden

Daniel E. Stetson, executive director, Polk Museum of Art, Lakeland, Fla.

Robert P. Sullivan, president, Bok Tower Gardens, Lake Wales, Fla.

Don Toeller, vice president of facilities, Museum of Science & Industry

Jeff Tucker, president & CEO, Tucker/Hall, Inc.

Renee Williams, director of arts and cultural affairs, City of Tampa

Nina Wolfson, Temple Terrace, Fla.

Gregory C. Yadley, attorney at law, Shumaker, Loop, & Kendrick LLP

Los Angeles Community Dialogue, December 11-12, 2000

LOCAL STEERING COMMITTEE

Irene Hirano (co-chair), executive director and president, Japanese American National Museum

Hon. Mark Ridley-Thomas (co-chair), member, Los Angeles City Council

Carlos Rafael Alvarado, senior deputy, City of Los Angeles

Nancy Araki, director, community affairs, Japanese American National Museum

Candace Barrett, executive director, Children's Museum of Los Angeles

Robert Barrett, vice president, domestic marketing, Los Angeles Convention & Visitors Bureau

Stephanie Barron, senior curator for modern and contemporary art, Los Angeles County Museum of Art

Tomas Benitez, director, Self Help Graphics and Art, Inc.

Adele Lander Burke, director of museum and education, Skirball Cultural Center

Marta de la Torre, director, information and communication, Getty Conservation Institute

William D. Estrada, curator, El Pueblo de Los Angeles Historical Monument

Mark Greenfield, director, Watts Towers Art Center

Jamesina E. Henderson, executive director, California African American Museum

Joe Hicks, executive director, Los Angeles City Human Relations Commission

Selma Holo, director, USC Fisher Gallery

Lela Hung, executive director, Community Partners

Jeanette LaVere, education and outreach coordinator, USC Fisher Gallery

Roella Hsieh Louie, arts manager, Los Angeles City Department of Cultural Affairs

Ted Mitchell, president, Occidental College

Mitchel D. Moore, executive director and founder, Heart of Los Angeles Youth

Leticia Quezada, director, Mexican Cultural Institute

Rashida Shah, program administrative assistant, Community Partners/Days of Dialogue

Jack Shakely, president, California Community Foundation

Fran Spears, executive director, National Conference for Community and Justice-Los Angeles

Marshall Wong, senior consultant, Los Angeles County Human Relations Commission

LOCAL STEERING COMMITTEE

Christy S. Coleman (co-chair), director, Charles H. Wright Museum of African American History

Steve Hamp (co-chair), president & CEO, Henry Ford Museum & Greenfield Village, Dearborn, Mich.

Ron L. Kagan (co-chair), director, Detroit Zoological Institute and Society

Susan Kelly (co-chair), senior manager, community relations, Target Corporation, East Zone, Minneapolis

Hashim Al-Tawil, cultural and educational coordinator, Arab-American and Chaldean Council Services

Blanca Almanza, vice president, corporate research, planning, and development, SER Metro-Detroit

Lucy Bukowski, deputy director, Cranbrook Institute of Science, Bloomfield Hills, Mich.

Larry C. Coppard, senior consultant, Community Foundation for Southeastern Michigan

Kathie D. Dones-Carson, director, City of Detroit

Haifa Fakhouri, president & CEO, Arab-American and Chaldean Council Services

Kenneth C. Fischer, executive director, University Musical Society, University of Michigan, Ann Arbor

Robert Ghannam, special events coordinator, Arab-American and Chaldean Council Services

Paul Hillegonds, president, Detroit Renaissance

Melvin J. Hollowell, Jr., partner, Butzel Long

Daniel H. Krichbaum, executive director, National Conference for Community and Justice-Detroit

Bridgett Lomax, program associate, Community Foundation for Southeastern Michigan

Heath Meriwether, publisher, Detroit Free Press

Susan T. Mosey, president, University Cultural Center Association

Talbert Spence, director, Cranbrook Institute of Science, Bloomfield Hills, Mich.

Shirley R. Stancato, president & CEO, New Detroit, Inc.

Paul E. Tait, executive director, Southeastern Michigan Council of Governments

Marilyn L. Wheaton, director, City of Detroit-Cultural Affairs

Wichita Community Dialogue, April 12, 2001

LOCAL STEERING COMMITTEE

Howard Ellington (co-chair), executive director, Wichita Center for the Arts

Robert A. Puckett (co-chair), director, Wichita-Sedgewick County Historical Museum

Charles K. Steiner (co-chair), director, Wichita Art Museum

Martin W. Bauer, attorney, Martin, Pringle, & Oliver Wallace & Swartz, LLP

Shirley Beggs, community volunteer

Vera Bothner, independent public relations consultant, Kansas Health Foundation

David Butler, director, Edwin A. Ulrich Museum of Art, Wichita State University

John D'Angelo, director, City Arts

Al Decena, president, Exploration Place

Larry Griffith, director, Birger Sandzén Memorial Gallery, Lindsborg, Kans.

Eric Key, director, Kansas African American Museum

Michael Michaelis, president & CEO, Emprise Financial Corporation

James D. Moore, director, Greater Wichita Community Foundation

Carol Nazar, director, Wichita Public Library

Gerald Norwood, account manager, Xerox Corporation

Douglas S. Pringle, senior vice president & trust officer, Commerce Bank

Paula Varner, community volunteer

Barbara Yarnell, director, Wichita Community Garden

LOCAL STEERING COMMITTEE

Ron Chew (co-chair), director, Wing Luke Asian Museum, Seattle

Jane A. Johnson (co-chair), CEO, Northwest Museum of Arts and Culture, Spokane

Thomas Livesay (co-chair), director, Whatcom Museum of History and Art

Teresa Brum, historic preservation officer, City/County Historic Preservation Office, Spokane

Don Drake, director, Whatcom Community Foundation

Dunham Gooding, board chair, Whatcom Museum of History and Art

Karen Marshall, director, Skagit County Historical Museum, La Conner, Wash.

Susan Parke, director, Museum of Northwest Art, La Conner, Wash.

Barbara Ryan, member, Bellingham City Council

Richard Vanderway, education and public programs coordinator, Whatcom Museum of History and Art

Scott Wallin, exhibit designer and curator, Whatcom Museum of History and Art

Bev Wilshire, operations manager, Whatcom Museum of History and Art

Tina Young, director, Office of Multicultural Initiatives, Seattle Central Community College

Kim Igoe, co-project director, Museums & Community, and vice president, policy & programs, AAM

Patricia E. Williams, co-project director, Museums & Community, and vice president & chief operating officer, Americans for the Arts, Washington, D.C.

Ingrid Denis, former program associate, policy & programs, AAM

Ellen Hirzy, consulting writer, Museums & Community

Jerold D Kappel, director of development, AAM

Jane Lusaka, editor, Museums & Community, and assistant director, publications, AAM

Maureen Robinson, project consultant and dialogue facilitator, Museums & Community

Alexandra Marmion Roosa, project manager, Museums & Community

David Thelen, observer/evaluator, Museums & Community, and professor of history, Indiana University, Bloomington

INDEX

· · · · ·

K

L

M

N

O

P